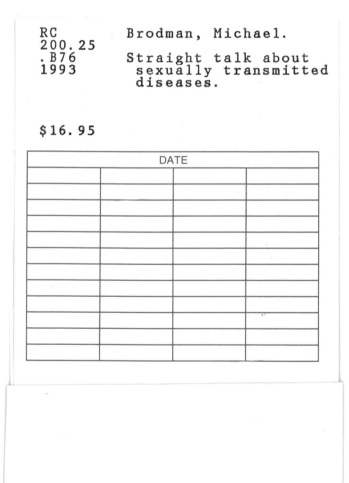

RC
200.25
.B76
1993

Brodman, Michael.

Straight talk about
sexually transmitted
diseases.

$16.95

DATE			

Straight Talk About Sexually Transmitted Diseases

Straight Talk About Sexually Transmitted Diseases

Michael Brodman, M.D.,
John Thacker and
Rachel Kranz

☑ Facts On File®

AN INFOBASE HOLDINGS COMPANY

Straight Talk About Sexually Transmitted Diseases

Facts On File, Inc.
460 Park Avenue South
New York, NY 10016

Library of Congress Cataloging-in-Publication Data
Brodman, Michael
    Straight talk about sexually transmitted diseases / Michael Brodman,
    John Thacker and Rachel Kranz.
        p.   cm.
    Includes index.
    Summary: Provides information about such sexually transmitted
    diseases as gonorrhea, syphilis, herpes, chlamydia, and AIDS, and how
    they can be prevented and treated.
        ISBN 0-8160-2864-8 (acid-free)
        1. Sexually transmitted diseases—Juvenile literature.
    [1. Sexually transmitted diseases.]   I. Kranz, Rachel.   II. Title.
    RC200.25.T43   1993
    616.95'1—dc20   93-20411

Facts On File books are available at special discounts when purchased in bulk quantities for businesses, associations, institutions, or sales promotions. Please contact our Special Sales Department in New York at 212/683-2244 or 800/322-8755.

Jacket design by Dorothy Wachtenheim

Printed in the United States of America

MP FOF 10 9 8 7 6 5 4 3 2

This book is printed on acid-free paper.

Contents

1

What Are Sexually Transmitted Diseases?

Elise and Martin* have been going out for about six months now. They both like each other a lot. Elise has gone out with a couple of other guys, but nothing this serious. Martin has never had a girlfriend before. So far, they've kissed and made out a lot. Now they think they're ready to go further—but they're both a little frightened.

Elise is nervous about getting pregnant. Martin knows that guys sometimes get infections from having sex. He has the impression that modern medicine can cure just

*All of the teenagers described in these scenarios are *composites*—portraits that combine many different features from various teenagers. None of them is an actual person.

1

about anything—but if he did get a sexually transmitted disease, what would he do? He can't really imagine going to the family doctor! They've both heard a lot about AIDS, which they know can't be cured. But since neither one of them is gay, do they really have to worry about that?

When it comes right down to it, Elise and Martin don't *really* think they've got anything to worry about. Still, just the idea of having sex for the first time makes them both nervous. And they still have a kind of nagging feeling that they might be doing something dangerous.

Charlie and Richard have been in a sexual relationship for about three months. Most of the time they don't even want to think about AIDS—so they don't. They certainly don't talk about it.

Nevertheless, they can't help thinking about it sometimes. Charlie is especially worried because he noticed that he was really tired and dragged out for a couple of weeks, running a fever, with pains in his legs and swollen glands. He read somewhere that these are early signs of AIDS. Or, it might just have been the flu. Charlie doesn't want to talk about his fears, because he thinks that will make them come true. Besides, now he's fine. That means everything's OK, doesn't it?

Robert and Marisol have been together for over a year. Although they feel close to each other and enjoy being together, they've never really talked much about their relationship. They've had sex together, and Marisol has taken birth-control pills, so they've never talked about either birth control or protection against STDs. Marisol hasn't gone out with any other guys since she and Robert started going together. She has taken it for granted that Robert hasn't gone out with any other girls, either. Then one day she is reading a magazine with a questionnaire about being at risk for STDs. One of the questions is, "Does your partner ever have relations with other people?" Marisol realizes that she doesn't really know the answer. She'd like to talk to Robert about it—but she doesn't know how to start.

Relationships: Choices and Responsibilities

Relationships can be one of the most satisfying aspects of life. Getting close to another person, physically as well as emotionally, can be an exciting and rewarding experience. Learning more about your own sexual feelings is one of the joys of becoming an adult.

Like most adult privileges, however, physical relationships bring responsibilities as well as pleasure. Beginning a physical relationship with another person means that you both have to make decisions about how far the relationship will go. Exactly what will you do to express your sexual feelings for each other? What do you do if one partner wants something that another partner isn't comfortable with or isn't ready for? Are there situations that might lead to your acting in a way that you may regret later? How can you work out your decisions with your partner—and how can you make sure that your decisions are completely right for you?

These questions concern your emotional well-being—the way you feel about yourself and your partner. But your feelings and your principles are not all you have to be concerned about. Your physical well-being—your health and safety—are also at stake. If a male and a female have sexual intercourse, they are risking the possibility that the female could get pregnant. And if any two people perform certain sexual acts, they may be risking exposure to sexually transmitted diseases (STDs).

The physical expression of romantic feelings is a wonderful part of life. In order to enjoy it fully, in the way that is right for you, you need to know as much as possible about all the consequences. This book will help you to become more informed about the possible physical consequences of sexual relationships. It will help you understand both the risks and some ways to lessen or prevent them. It will also offer some concrete suggestions about how to talk things over with a partner and how to think things through on your own.

The more informed you are about sex and its consequences, the better decisions you'll be able to make for yourself—and the more pleasure you'll get from whatever decisions you make. Let's start our discussion with a short quiz on STDs, so that you can see just how much you know about this important subject.

STDs: Facts vs. Myths

How much do you know about sexually transmitted diseases? Identify the following statements as **Fact** or **Myth**. Then read on to find out whether you were right.

____ 1. A person can only get one STD at a time.

____ 2. Once you've gotten an STD, you can't get the same disease again.

____ 3. It's possible to get an STD even if you don't have sexual intercourse.

____ 4. You can't get an STD from a toilet, from sharing food, or from someone's cough or sneeze.

____ 5. A virgin can't get an STD; the first time is always safe.

____ 6. A good condom will remain effective for more than one sexual act.

____ 7. A person can get an STD from someone who isn't even sick.

____ 8. You can always tell someone with a sexually transmitted disease—they look dirty or unhealthy.

____ 9. Only gay men (men who have intercourse with other men) get AIDS.

____10. If you and your partner have both tested negative for AIDS, it's safe to have sex without a condom.

1. A person can only get one STD at a time.—Myth. Getting one type of sexually transmitted disease provides no *immunity* (protection) against getting any other disease. In fact, having unprotected sex (oral, vaginal, or anal intercourse without a condom) exposes you to a number of diseases. The more often you do it, and the more people you do it with, the greater the risk. If your partner has had other partners, you're also risking exposure to any disease that any of these partners may have had. The more people in the sexual "network" of unprotected sex, the wider the variety of STDs to which you're exposed. Under those circumstances, the chances of contracting more than one STD go up.

2. Once you've gotten an STD, you can't get the same disease again.—Myth. STDs aren't like measles or chicken pox. Some of them can be cured, and some of them can't—but only one of them—hepatitis B—gives you immunity. All the others, especially syphilis and gonorrhea, you can get again and again. A person who has unprotected sex, especially with more than one partner, is more likely to risk exposure to an STD—and so is more likely to catch the same disease two or more times.

3. It's possible to get an STD even if you don't have sexual intercourse.—Fact. Sexual intercourse—the penetration of the vagina by the penis—may be one of the most likely ways to contract an STD, but it isn't the only one. Some STDs can be transmitted through kissing. Other risky activities are oral sex (mouth to penis or mouth to vagina) and anal sex (penis to *anus* [rear opening]). Stopping a sexual act halfway through won't provide any protection from a sexually transmitted disease: if you've had the kinds of contact described without a condom, you've been exposed.

AIDS can also be contracted through sharing the needle of an infected person or through receiving a transfusion of infected blood. (However, you can't get AIDS through *giving* blood.)

4. You can't get an STD from a toilet, from sharing food, or from someone's cough or sneeze.—Fact. Sexually transmitted diseases are passed on by intimate contact. They aren't like the flu or a cold. If you know someone with an STD, you can feel free to spend time with that person without risk of infection. Only sexual contact—mouth-to-mouth kissing, or oral, anal, or genital sex—will expose you to the disease.

5. A virgin can't get an STD; the first time is always safe.—Myth. Anyone who has been exposed to a sexually transmitted disease is at risk. It's true that the more often you are exposed, the more likely you are to catch the disease. But saying that you can't get an STD if you're a virgin is like saying that you can't get hit the first time you run out onto a crowded freeway. You *might* be lucky enough to get across once—but you'd be foolish to count on it.

6. A good condom will remain effective for more than one sexual act.—Myth. Because condoms are one of the best protections against STDs, it's important to know exactly how to use them effectively. A condom can only be used once. After the male *ejaculates* (comes), the condom needs to be taken off and replaced before he comes again. It isn't safe for the male to stay inside the female or another male and come a second or third time wearing the same condom. Nor is it safe to use the same condom for oral sex (mouth to penis) and then vaginal sex (penis to vagina) or anal sex (penis to anus). To be effective, a condom can only be used once—that is, the male can only come into it one time.

7. A person can get an STD from someone who isn't even sick.—Fact. Some people are *carriers* of sexually transmitted disease. That means that they have been exposed to the disease and have contracted the virus or bacteria that causes it, but they aren't experiencing any symptoms themselves at the moment. Nevertheless, they are fully capable of passing the virus or bacteria on to a sexual partner.

Many STDs come in stages. A person might get symptoms for a few weeks, then see the symptoms disappear. This does *not* mean that the disease has gone away or "cured itself." It means that the disease has gone deeper into the person's body and is likely to come back with even stronger symptoms a few weeks, months, or even years later. The person may still be able to infect other people and is taking terrible risks as well.

8. You can always tell someone with a sexually transmitted disease—they look dirty or unhealthy.— Myth. As we've seen, cleanliness has nothing to do with STDs and how they are transmitted. Neither does "looking healthy." In many cases, AIDS has an *incubation* (growth) period of up to 10 years. That means that a person can have the virus that causes AIDS for up to 10 years without showing any symptoms. All that time, however, the infected person is exposing his or her sexual partners to the disease. There's no way to tell just by looking.

Likewise, mild symptoms of syphilis and gonorrhea may show up right after the disease has been contracted and then disappear for some time before coming back in a more severe form. For all the time that the infected person has no symptoms, however, he or she is still carrying around the disease—and is still capable of passing it on to others.

Some STDs, like genital herpes and genital warts, have no visible symptoms outside the genital area. Genital warts are associated with cancer and *sterility* (not being able to have children), and herpes can cause problems for women when giving birth. But none of this is visible to the naked eye. Even the herpes sores and genital warts might not be visible.

Chlamydia is another disease that may be "silent"—without visible symptoms. Generally, STDs are more likely to be silent in women than in men, so the only way a woman might know if she had been exposed to a disease is if her male partner told her about his symptoms.

Because sexually transmitted diseases are so frightening, it might be comforting to believe that "normal" people don't get them, that being clean and otherwise healthy is some protection, or that these are diseases only poor people get. It might be comforting—but it isn't true. Anyone who has been exposed to a sexually transmitted disease can get one and can pass it on to others.

9. Only gay men (men who have intercourse with other men) get AIDS.—Myth. Anyone who has been exposed to the AIDS virus can get AIDS. Although one of the most common ways of being exposed is through homosexual sex, many "straight" men have contracted AIDS from sex with women who were infected. Likewise, many women have contracted AIDS from sex with infected men. If these women become pregnant, their children might also be infected with the AIDS virus. And, of course, anyone who shares a needle with or receives a blood transfusion from someone with AIDS is at risk, no matter what his or her sexual preference.

When AIDS was first discovered in the United States, it seemed to be a disease that occurred primarily among gay men, *hemophiliacs* (people with a heredity blood disorder requiring frequent infusions of blood clotting factors), and drug users who shared needles. This led to the thinking that there were certain high-risk *groups*. The thinking was that if you belonged to one of these groups, you were at greater risk than others.

As AIDS has become more widespread, however, the thinking has changed. Now the experts talk about high-risk *behaviors*. That means that anyone who acts in a certain way is putting himself or herself at risk, no matter which group he or she belongs to. *Anyone* who has sex without a condom is taking the risk of getting AIDS.

10. If you and your partner have both tested negative for AIDS, it's safe to have sex without a condom.— Myth. You can be tested to find out whether you have AIDS.

However, the test isn't foolproof. Sometimes it takes six months or so after infection for the test to reveal the presence of antibodies for the disease. So even if you and your partner have both tested negative, one of you might still be putting the other at risk for at least six months after the test.

In addition, if either partner engages in high-risk behavior (genital, anal, or oral sex) with somebody else, he or she is opening up a new chance for infection. Even having sex once with an infected person puts you at risk. If your partner has sex with someone else only once, that puts you at risk, too. If you don't use condoms, you're exposing yourself to these risks.

Back to Basics

Now that you've checked up on your own knowledge, let's go back and review the facts. In Chapter 2, we'll describe the eight major sexually transmitted diseases, their treatments, and how you can tell whether you or someone else has one. That information will be easier to understand, though, if we start with some basic information about human sexual organs and behavior.

Sometimes reading, thinking, or talking about sex makes people uncomfortable. Some people find it exciting or kind of a turn on. Other people feel disgusted, turned off, nervous, or upset. Many people have several reactions—one after the other or all at the same time!

Even sexually experienced adults often have trouble thinking about sex, so it's no wonder that teenagers, even sexually experienced ones, tend to feel uncomfortable. But if you don't know the facts about sex, you won't know how to take care of yourself and the people you care about.

In Chapters 5 and 6, we'll offer some suggestions for talking about sex with friends, parents, and boyfriends or girlfriends. For now, if you're uncomfortable reading about the topic, we suggest that you find a way to pay attention to your feelings without letting them keep you from getting the information that you need. Notice what makes you uncomfortable and keep on reading. If you have to, take a break. Maybe it would help to find a private place to read, or maybe you'd be more comfortable reading in a public, anonymous place, like a library or a coffee shop. It might also help to find someone to talk to about what you're reading—a friend, a sympathetic adult, or even a voice on the other end of a hot line (Chapters 5 and 7 have some suggestions for finding people to talk to). Whatever you do, though, don't give up! Information about your body and other people's bodies is important to your life and your health—so keep reading until you've found out everything that you need to know.

The Woman's Body

Women have *genitals* (sexual organs) both inside and outside their bodies. The *external*, or outside, organs are called the *vulva*. The vulva includes several parts that surround or cover the opening to the *vagina*, which leads inside the woman's body to the *internal* (inside) sexual organs. (Take a look at the diagrams to help you follow this description.)

The opening of the vagina is protected by two sets of "lips"—a big set called *labia majora* (Latin for "big lips") and a smaller set underneath called *labia minora* (Latin for "small lips"). At the top of the vagina's opening is the *clitoris*, a small organ about the size of a raisin. the clitoris is the source of women's sexual pleasure, the way the penis is the source of men's sexual pleasure. When a woman has an orgasm or "comes," it's usually because her clitoris has been rubbed or stimulated in some way, either directly, by touching or kissing, or indirectly, by the movement of the penis, finger, or tongue inside the vagina. However, many women find the whole area of the vulva to be an area of sexual pleasure and enjoy being touched or kissed in many places there.

There is another opening in this region of a woman's body, known as the *urethra*. The urethra leads to the woman's bladder and is the opening through which she

Female Reproductive System

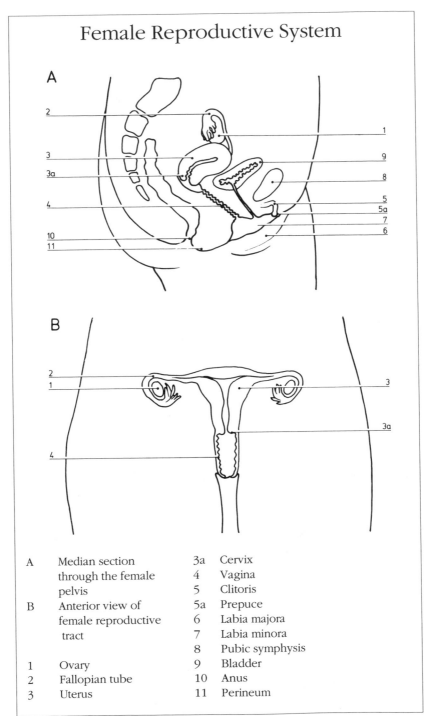

A   Median section   3a   Cervix
      through the female   4   Vagina
      pelvis   5   Clitoris
B   Anterior view of   5a   Prepuce
      female reproductive   6   Labia majora
      tract   7   Labia minora
                              8   Pubic symphysis
1   Ovary   9   Bladder
2   Fallopian tube   10   Anus
3   Uterus   11   Perineum

urinates, or pees. The urethra is a very tiny opening, unlike the vagina, which in a sexually mature woman is large enough for a penis to be inserted into or for a baby to be born out of.

The vagina leads into the inside of a woman's body, into her *uterus,* or womb. When a woman gets pregnant, the baby grows inside her uterus.

The *fallopian tubes* connect the uterus to the *ovaries*—the female organs that produce human eggs. One day every month, the ovaries release an egg into a fallopian tube, a time that is called *ovulation.* (Many women have a special vaginal discharge during this time.) If during ovulation some male *sperm* (seed) travels through the vagina, up into the uterus and the fallopian tubes, a woman's egg is likely to become fertilized and the woman becomes pregnant.

Every month, the uterus is lined with nourishment for a potential fertilized egg. If a woman does not get pregnant, the lining falls away and comes out through the vaginal opening. That's what happens when a woman *menstruates,* or gets her period. That's why missing a period is often the sign that a woman is pregnant. (However, a woman can miss a period or have a late period for lots of other reasons, including stress, excessive dieting, or some other medical problem. And sometimes a pregnant woman can have one or even two periods, as some but not all of the uterus's lining falls away. (That means a woman might be two or even three months pregnant before she misses a period.)

As you can see, women's *fertility,* or ability to get pregnant, goes in a monthly cycle. First the lining on the walls of the uterus builds up, getting ready to nourish a potential baby. Then the woman ovulates, producing eggs and releasing them into the fallopian tubes. If an egg is fertilized during this time, the woman gets pregnant. If not, the lining of the uterus comes out as a monthly period. Then the lining starts to build up once more—and the whole process starts again.

You might assume from this information that the only time a woman can get pregnant is during ovulation, when eggs

External Female Genitals

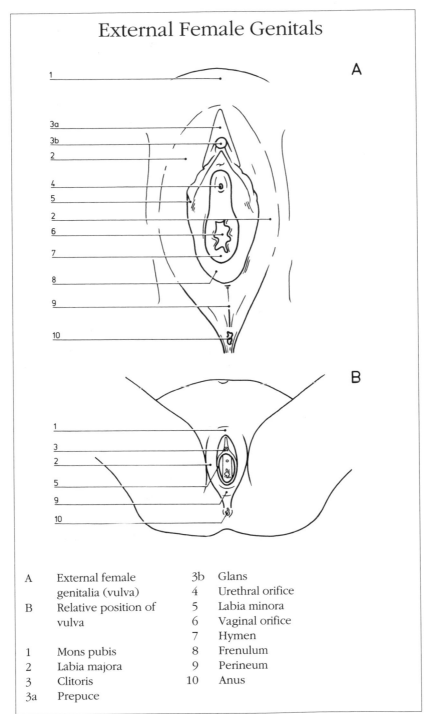

A	External female genitalia (vulva)	3b	Glans
B	Relative position of vulva	4	Urethral orifice
		5	Labia minora
		6	Vaginal orifice
		7	Hymen
1	Mons pubis	8	Frenulum
2	Labia majora	9	Perineum
3	Clitoris	10	Anus
3a	Prepuce		

are produced and released. Technically, this is true. In fact, this information is the basis of the rhythm method, in which a woman keeps track of her monthly period to calculate which days are "safe"—that is, which days she is not ovulating. Some women believe that if they have sex only on the days when they are not ovulating, they won't be able to get pregnant.

There are problems with this assumption however. It is difficult for a woman to be certain in advance on which day she is ovulating. Many women and most teenagers are not completely "regular." Some months, there may be 10 days between the last day of their periods and the day they start ovulating. Some months, there may be nine days, or eight, or 12, or 14. It's difficult to be completely certain. And because a woman's body is, in a sense, designed to get pregnant, making a mistake is almost certain to lead to pregnancy.

No time of the month is completely "safe" from the possibility of getting pregnant. The only way to be sure to avoid pregnancy is to avoid sex altogether and to keep sperm far away from the vaginal opening. Using some physical means of birth control is a good idea, for several reasons, but no method of birth control except abstinence is foolproof. (For more about birth control, see Chapter 5.)

Another part of the female body that's important to know about is the *cervix*. The cervix is actually the lower part of the uterus—a narrow canal that leads from the vagina into the bigger part of the uterus. This canal is surrounded by a bony area that protects the narrow opening. If a woman puts her finger deep into her vagina, she can feel a hard area at the very end. That's the cervix. When a woman uses a *diaphragm* (a small rubber cup that is used for birth control), she inserts it into her vagina until it covers the opening to her cervix and she can feel the hard area behind it.

The Man's Body

A man's external sexual organs are the *penis* and the two *testes*. The testes hang inside a small sack, called the *scrotum*. They are very tender and sensitive. Some men enjoy having

Male Reproductive System

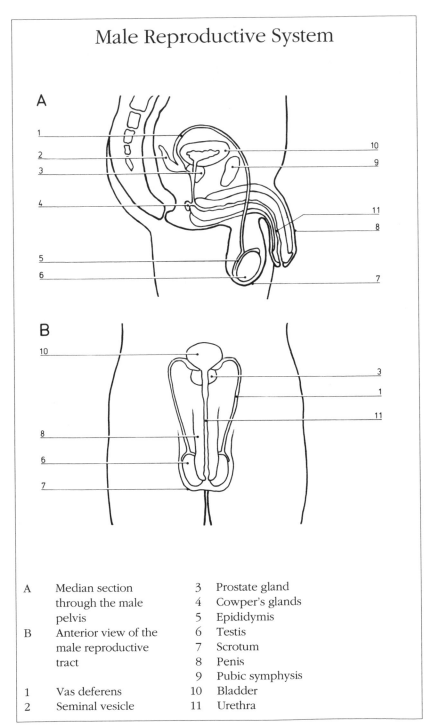

A	Median section through the male pelvis	3	Prostate gland
		4	Cowper's glands
		5	Epididymis
B	Anterior view of the male reproductive tract	6	Testis
		7	Scrotum
		8	Penis
		9	Pubic symphysis
1	Vas deferens	10	Bladder
2	Seminal vesicle	11	Urethra

them touched or kissed gently, but having them squeezed or pressed is very painful. The testes manufacture the man's *sperm*, or seed, as well as the male hormone, *testosterone*.

The penis hangs in front of the scrotum. Most of the time, the penis is fairly small and hangs down limply, but when the man is sexually *aroused*, or excited, the penis becomes stiffer, thicker, and gradually points up or straight ahead. This is known as having an *erection*.

At birth, the tip of the penis is covered with a small layer of skin called the *foreskin*. In some cultures and religions, the foreskin is removed when the male child is still an infant in a procedure known as *circumcision*.

Many myths surround circumcision, including that removing the foreskin makes the penis less sensitive or prevents masturbation. None of these myths is true. Circumcision has no effect on the sensitivity of the penis and does not affect sexual performance or masturbation one way or another. It's true that dirt may accumulate under the foreskin, but if a boy is taught to draw back the foreskin and clean it, an uncircumcised penis is just as clean as a circumcised one.

If a penis has not been circumcised, the foreskin peels back by itself as the penis becomes erect, exposing the head of the penis. The scientific name for this part of the body is the *glans penis*. This part of the body is extremely sensitive in men, just as the clitoris is sensitive in women. Both organs are full of nerve receptors, which is what causes the intense physical feelings during sexual intercourse or masturbation.

Just under the glans is a little band of tissue called the *frenulum*, which keeps the foreskin from peeling back completely. The frenulum is also a very sensitive area. The third sensitive area on the penis is the ridge running underneath it, along the *shaft*, or body, or the penis.

In the center of the glans is the man's urethra. As with the woman, the urethra is the opening through which he urinates. The man's urethra runs inside the center of the penis into the bladder, where *urine* (pee) is stored.

Male Genitals

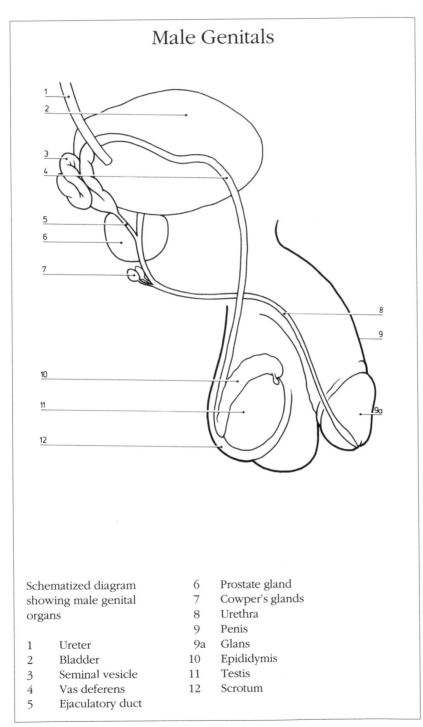

Schematized diagram
showing male genital
organs

1	Ureter
2	Bladder
3	Seminal vesicle
4	Vas deferens
5	Ejaculatory duct
6	Prostate gland
7	Cowper's glands
8	Urethra
9	Penis
9a	Glans
10	Epididymis
11	Testis
12	Scrotum

The man's urethra is also connected to his *prostate*, a gland inside his body that manufactures a liquid that helps nourish sperm during intercourse. Many tiny ducts connect the prostate to the urethra.

Behind the prostate, still inside the man's body, are two pouches called the *seminal vesicles*, which hold the sticky fluid that contains a man's sperm during intercourse. These seminal vesicles feed into the prostate and the urethra on one end; at the other end, they are connected to tubes called *vas deferens*, which in turn connect to the testes, where sperm is stored. If a man grasps the scrotum where it joins his body and rolls the tissues gently with the thumb in front and the index finger behind, he can feel a cordlike structure—the vas deferens.

During sexual intercourse, liquid from the prostate, fluid from the seminal vesicles, and sperm from the testes all pass through the vas deferens into the urethra and out the opening at the end of the penis. That happens when the man *ejaculates*, or comes.

Not So Different

Although we have described the sexual organs of men and women in detail that makes them seem fairly different, in fact, these organs have a lot more in common than we might think. After all, during the first six weeks in the womb, male and female fetuses look identical.

Then, when male and female organs do begin to develop, each male organ develops from the same type of tissue as the female organ that "matches" it. And each male organ has the same function as the female organ that matches it. Some organs' function is to produce sperm or eggs in order to continue reproduction. Some body parts' job is to protect sensitive areas. Others have the function of providing pleasure.

Although scientists are still studying the biological differences between men and women, they are sure of two things: both men and women have a role to play in creating children; and both men and women have a strong drive to have sex and to enjoy sexual pleasure. As human beings, we have lots of choices about how to handle our feelings and sexual desires, including deciding not to have sex. As teenagers, we may experience sexual interest at different times or to different extents, depending on our age, upbringing, and situation. What we all have in common may be greater than our differences, however.

What Happens During Sex

As men and women start to get sexually excited, veins in the vulva, clitoris, and penis begin to *dilate* (open) and fill with blood. Filling with blood makes the penis stiffen and become erect. The clitoris has a similar reaction. Both men and women secrete various fluids, the man through the urethra's opening in the penis, the woman from the vagina.

As sexual excitement builds, men find their penises getting harder, stiffer, and more erect. Women find themselves getting "wetter" as the vagina swells with blood and produces fluid. This vaginal fluid is an early sign of sexual excitement in women. It also helps to *lubricate* (moisten) the vaginal area so that women who have sex with men can more easily receive the penis.

In sex between men and women, the man might insert his penis into the woman's vagina, where rubbing it back and forth stimulates both the shaft and the tip of the penis while indirectly stimulating the clitoris.

A couple might also have *oral sex*, kissing each other's genitals. They might engage in *mutual masturbation*, where each touches the other's genitals in ways that the person finds pleasurable. Or they might have *anal sex*, in which the man inserts his penis into the woman's anus. The couple might continue until one or both has an *orgasm* (see below) or feels satisfied in some other way.

Men having sex together likewise might have oral sex, anal sex, or masturbate each other; women having sex together might engage in oral sex, mutual masturbation, or rubbing their genital areas against each other. The peak of sexual excitement is known as the *orgasm* (coming). In men, orgasm happens along with *ejaculation*—the release of a sticky stream of *semen*, including sperm and the fluid that nourishes it. Men's orgasm can happen from the penis being touched, kissed, inserted into a vagina, or inserted into an anus.

Women's orgasm happens from stimulation to the clitoris (only 20 percent of women achieve orgasm with intercourse alone). Some women enjoy the sensation of a penis, a finger, or a tongue inside their vagina, but stimulation to the vagina is usually not as important to the woman's orgasm as stimulating (touching, kissing, or rubbing against) her clitoris. When a woman reaches orgasm, like a man, her muscles contract, and then release. She can especially feel the muscles of her vagina contracting and releasing.

Besides the physical pleasure that orgasm brings, it has a biological function: to create a future child. If a man's penis is inside a woman's vagina, his ejaculation sends sperm along the vaginal tract and into her uterus. If the woman reaches orgasm, her vaginal contractions help send the sperm into the uterus, where it might fertilize an egg. It's important for both men and women to remember that everything about their bodies is designed to produce pregnancy; that's why it's so important to use birth control if you have sex and don't want pregnancy to occur. It's also important to know that a woman can get pregnant whether she has an orgasm or not, and that a man may release some sperm into a woman's body even if he does not have an orgasm. Thus the woman can get pregnant even if the couple starts to have intercourse and then stops before either one comes.

In both sexes, getting sexually aroused without reaching orgasm can feel somewhat uncomfortable or painful. However, this is not a dangerous state in any way. Either men or women can relieve the pain by masturbating—bringing themselves to orgasm. Men who are aroused without reaching orgasm are likely to have *nocturnal emissions*—that is, they will have an orgasm and an ejaculation at night, while they are sleeping. Either a man or a woman might find it frustrating to kiss, pet, or make out without "going all the way," but this frustration is not dangerous. Nor is it any reason to put pressure on another person to have sexual intercourse.

How Diseases Can Be Passed on through Sex

As we have seen, both men and women's bodies have a number of openings: the anus and urethra in men and women; the vagina in women. In both men and women, the friction of having sex can create tiny, invisible *abrasions*, or scrapes, through which infections can pass into the bloodstream. In both male and female sex organs, a number of ducts and vessels connect the bladder and the genitals. In men, the prostate and the testes are also connected to this system; in women, the ovaries and cervix are connected.

What this means is that there are plenty of places that an infection—either a bacteria or a virus—can be introduced into a man's or a woman's body. And when an infection is introduced into either a man or a woman, it has plenty of places to spread.

For example, during vaginal intercourse, the man's penis rubs against the woman's labia, causing tiny, invisible abrasions. The bacteria that causes syphilis might be transferred from the penis to the woman's labia during intercourse; the virus that causes AIDS might also pass from the man's semen into the woman's bloodstream.

If the bacteria that causes gonorrhea enters the woman's urethra during intercourse, it can linger inside her body for a long time if it isn't treated. The lingering bacteria can also then infect a person who has sex with her.

When a person contracts syphilis, the germs form a tiny *ulcer*, or sore, often on the vulva or penis. However, a woman might not even know she is sick for a long time. Meanwhile, the disease gets worse—and her next sexual partner may become infected. The lining of the cervix can be infected by either chlamydia or gonorrhea, and again, those diseases can then linger to infect the woman's next partner.

Gonorrhea, chlamydia, and some other STDs can also spread throughout women's sexual organs to infect the fallopian tubes or the ovaries, which can cause sterility by blocking the fallopian tubes.

In men, the bacteria that cause syphilis can enter the penis through tiny, invisible abrasions in the foreskin, the skin covering the penis, or the skin covering the glans or the frenulum. As in women, men's urethras are connected to other sexual organs, which means that gonorrhea and chlamydia bacteria can pass into that area as well.

Anal sex is an especially risky form of intercourse, because the penis rubbing against the walls of the anus is so much more likely to cause abrasions, allowing bacteria and viruses entry into the bloodstream. People who practice anal sex should be especially sure to use condoms to help prevent infection.

2

The Eight Major Sexually Transmitted Diseases

Elise and Martin figure out a time and place that they can be alone together for a few hours. Without really saying anything about it, they know they are going to have sex. Both are very excited and looking forward to their first time together—but both are still feeling kind of nervous. Elise wonders whether Martin will bring a condom, or whether he'll just assume that she has birth control. She doesn't want to get pregnant, but she can't imagine how she'll ever be able to talk to him about "doing it." She hopes that if she just doesn't think about it, somehow, things will work out.

She also wonders what having sex will be like. She's heard that it hurts the first time, and she wonders how badly it hurts and whether she's supposed to act like it doesn't. Or, if it doesn't hurt, will Martin think she's not a virgin and look down on her? What if she doesn't enjoy it and he thinks she's frigid? What if she enjoys it a lot and he thinks she's a slut? She's really liked everything she and Martin have done together so far, but she's heard that sex itself is different. Some of the sexual things she's heard or read about sound pretty gross.

Martin worries about doing things the right way. He knows it's Elise's first time, too, but he still thinks that she will be able to judge whether he's a good lover or not. What if he can't get hard at the right time? What if he can't stay hard? What if he comes too soon—or what if he takes too long to come? He loves Elise, but he knows he could never talk to her about his worries—no way.

As much as he doesn't want to worry, Charlie finds himself going over and over those two weeks when he felt so sick. Were his glands extra swollen, or was he just a little sore? Did he really have pains in his legs, or was he just tired and achy from the flu? Or maybe he pulled a muscle somehow? The more he thinks about it, the more frantic he gets, until he finds he can't think about anything else.

Charlie decides to put an end to his worries by getting tested for AIDS. He doesn't want to talk to anyone about his fears—no one but Richard even knows he's gay. But he calls a hot-line number that he sees on a bus, because the ad says it's confidential. Charlie finds out that he can get tested confidentially, so that no one but him will know he went. The person on the hot line explains that the test is just a simple blood test.

Charlie is so relieved at the idea that he can put an end to his worries that he tells Richard about his plans to get tested. Much to his surprise, Richard freaks out. He tells Charlie that he doesn't believe the test results are really secret—somehow they'll get back to Charlie's parents and his school. "Is that what you want?" Richard says. "Besides, what difference does it make? If you've got AIDS, you've got it. If you don't, you don't. You're not going to stop having sex, are you? You just have to go ahead and keep taking the risk."

When Marisol is having her regular doctor's checkup, she discovers she has PID—pelvic inflammatory disease. The doctor explains that this disease might not be serious right now, but that Marisol has had it for a long time without knowing it, and that it might have bad consequences later. The doctor can give her medicine for it now, but Marisol should know that the disease might have injured her fallopian tubes. In other words, the doctor explains, Marisol might have trouble getting pregnant and having a baby.

Marisol has always wanted children, and the news makes her very upset. She had one boyfriend before Robert, and she had sex with him a couple of times before they eventually broke up. the doctor has explained that she probably got the PID from having sex with someone. Marisol doesn't know whether it was from Robert or from her old boyfriend. Has she passed on some kind of disease to Robert? Is her old boyfriend passing it on to his new girlfriend? She doesn't want to talk about it with anyone, but she knows she has to.

Knowing the Facts

Now that you have a general idea of how diseases might be transmitted through sexual contact, let's look at the most common sexually transmitted diseases in the United States. Following is information on eight major sexually transmitted diseases: what they are, how they are contracted, what their symptoms are, where they can lead, and how they can be treated.*

---

*All statistics except those for AIDS are from the Centers for Disease Control's records for 1991, the latest year for which data is available; AIDS data comes from the CDC's February 1993 report.

Some of these diseases are more common than others. Some have relatively simple cures; others have complicated cures; still others have no cure at all. But all of these diseases have one thing in common: they can all be prevented if you know how to do it and are willing to take the time and trouble to take care of yourself.

Chlamydia

Although many people have never even heard of it, chlamydia is the nation's most common sexually transmitted disease: 4 million annual U.S. cases. Both men and women can get chlamydia, but the results are far more serious for women, who might lose their ability to have children.

Although chlamydia can have such serious results, it may exist without any symptoms at all. About one-fourth of all men and one-half of all women who have it don't have any way of knowing about it unless they get tested for it. Doctors recommend that those women in the groups listed below be tested for chlamydia at least once a year. In fact, anyone in the following categories should get tested for chlamydia:

1. Women and heterosexual men who have another STD.
2. Women who have evidence of PID or some other infection.
3. Women or men who have had more than one sexual partner.
4. Heterosexual men who have a painful or unusual discharge from the penis.
5. Homosexual men who have infections or inflammations in the anal area that aren't due to gonorrhea or genital herpes.

Chlamydia is actually a fairly new disease—only 25 years old—but it has been spreading with alarming speed. You might also see it referred to as "non-gonococcal genital infection" (that is, a genital infection that isn't caused by the

bacteria that cause gonorrhea), or NGGI. Actual
of different organisms might cause this conditi
the most common cause is the bacteria calle
trachomatis.

If a man gets chlamydia, his urethra is infected and his
penis may have an unusual discharge. He will generally
notice this between one and two weeks after infection. The
man might also have difficulty or pain while urinating. Or,
he may have no symptoms at all.

If the organism spreads to the man's bladder (where urine
is stored) or prostate, he may feel more discomfort and pain,
especially while urinating. However, this spread may also
have no symptoms for a while.

If chlamydia isn't treated in men, they may go on to develop
more serious diseases, including swellings in the joints as in
arthritis. A man may also get urethritis (a disease of the urethra)
or conjunctivitis (an inflammation of the eyes).

Women are affected in the cervix or in other parts of the
genital tract. When women are infected in the cervix, they don't
have any visible symptoms and may easily infect men through
contact between the penis and the cervix. In the same way, a
man with chlamydia might infect a woman's cervix.

Women with chlamydia may get pelvic inflammatory
disease (PID), which as we will see, might lead to not being
able to have children. (For other effects of PID, see the
section below.) A woman having even one serious chlamydia infection has a 12 percent chance of having damage to
her fallopian tubes that can lead to infertility; a woman who
is infected twice has a 40 percent chance of becoming
infertile; a woman infected three times has an 80 percent
chance of infertility.

The best way to prevent chlamydia is always to use a
condom, diaphragm, and spermicide during heterosexual
intercourse, and always to use a condom and spermicide
during male homosexual intercourse. If a man is having a
discharge from his penis, he should have it investigated and
not have sex until he's found out whether or not he has

chlamydia. If a woman is experiencing any of the symptoms of PID (see below), she should do the same.

Chlamydia can be treated with antibiotics. Doctors may need to make tests to make sure what is causing the problem.

Gonorrhea

This sexually transmitted disease has been easily treated by antibiotics in the past, but new strains are emerging that resist medication.

The bacteria that cause gonorrhea—the *gonococcus*—grow in moist, warm areas: the mouth, throat, rectum, urinary tract, and cervix. However, as with other STDs, a person might have gonorrhea for some time and not realize it, because the symptoms are often so faint and so easily mistaken for something else.

Men and women have different symptoms for gonorrhea. This is one of those STDs that makes it clear why trust and communication between partners is so important: It is much easier for men to tell they have gonorrhea than it is for women. And gonorrhea is highly *contagious* (easy to pass on), so the chances are good that if you have sex with someone who's infected, you will get it, too. A woman whose male partner has gonorrhea needs to hear about it from him right away, so that she can get herself tested and, if necessary, treated. (Of course, a man whose female partner has gonorrhea, or any other STD, also needs to hear about it from her! For more on talking to partners, see Chapter 5.)

A man starts getting gonorrhea symptoms from three to five days after he has been exposed. His urethra will start to tingle or feel uncomfortable, and he will feel a burning sensation in his urethra while urinating. Soon afterward, a thick, creamy, bad-smelling discharge will drip from his penis, and the area around the "eye" of his penis will be red.

Although these are pretty clear symptoms, it's important to know that the man won't have any other problems. Gonorrhea can eventually be quite serious, but at this early stage, it doesn't feel like a major illness.

About a week or two later, if the man hasn't gotten treatment, the infection spreads upward into his urethra, inflaming the part near the bladder (the organ that holds a person's urine). As a result, the burning and pain of urination get worse. The man may also feel sicker than he did before, suffering from headaches or fever caused by the poisonous substances in his bloodstream. However, even this stage of sickness may not feel like more than a bout of the flu.

If the man has still not gotten treatment, he may not have any more symptoms for a long time—or the disease may spread to nearby organs, such as the prostate, the bladder, or the testes. If the disease does get into the testes, it causes them to feel painful and swollen; gonorrhea here might cause permanent sterility.

Some men may not even experience the symptoms described here, although this is fairly rare. Whether or not a person is experiencing symptoms, however, he or she is still *infectious* (capable of passing on a disease).

If gonorrhea isn't treated, it may turn into *chronic* (permanent) gonorrhea. Men with chronic gonorrhea suffer from the urethra *constricting*, or getting narrow, which makes it very painful and difficult to urinate.

Sometimes a man has symptoms that are similar to gonorrhea but are actually produced by a disease called *nongonococcal urethritis* (NGU), another type of infection of the urethra. This disease also produces a discharge, but is caused—and therefore cured—differently from gonorrhea. Also, sometimes men have discharges from their penises that aren't caused by either of these diseases.

It's possible for a man to have any unusual discharges tested and then *diagnosed* (analyzed to see what the cause is) in the same day. A man who notices discharge from his penis should get it checked as soon as possible and should not have genital sex with anyone until he's sure that he's healthy. A woman or a man who notices discharge from a partner's penis should not have sex with the person until he has been tested and, if necessary, cured.

Women suffer much milder symptoms when they first get gonorrhea—and risk much greater health problems if the disease continues to go untreated. Some 30 percent to 50 percent of infected women have no symptoms of gonorrhea. If a woman's male partner doesn't tell her that he is infected, either because he isn't trustworthy or because he himself doesn't know, she might contract the disease and never know it. At that point, she is a danger both to herself and to any man who has sex with her without a condom. Women who have sexual intercourse with men without a condom—especially if they have ever had more than one partner, and most especially if they have more than one partner within the same period of time—should get regular tests for gonorrhea. (Of course, a much better protection against gonorrhea for heterosexually active women is to always have your male partner wear a condom and to only have sex with men whom you trust to check themselves for symptoms and tell you about them.)

Even when women do develop symptoms of gonorrhea, they are less obvious than men's, and they tend to last for a shorter time. That's because the urethra is the place where gonorrhea germs "hide out," and women's urethras are much shorter than men's. Their shorter urethras are also more easily cleaned out by the passing of urine. Thus, the pain in the woman's urethra may end—but the gonorrhea can still spread to other parts of her body. By the time the woman does feel significant pain, she may already have a very serious infection. Some 40 percent to 60 percent of the women who do have gonorrhea symptoms don't notice them because they are so mild; or they mistake the symptoms for something else.

If a woman does get early symptoms of gonorrhea, they'll usually appear from two days to three weeks after having been exposed. Most commonly, women are infected in the cervix. Like men, they experience a discharge, caused by an irritating substance released by the bacteria when they die. The discharge may take a while to work its way down from the cervix through the vagina, or it may never show up outside the woman's body. Inside the woman's body, on her cervix, there may be redness, small bumps, or other physical signs, but a woman can't see these without a *speculum* (an instrument that has a mirror on it, allowing a woman to look inside her body). A woman who takes the pill might confuse reactions to the pill with gonorrhea symptoms.

Another female symptom is a burning sensation in the urethra, especially when urinating, caused by the urethra being infected. However, as we have seen, the first signs of the infection may be "washed away" by urination and not be noticed.

If a woman has gonorrhea and isn't treated, the infection might spread to Skene's glands (which are on each side of the opening through which she urinates) and Bartholin's glands (two glands inside the vagina that release the fluid that appears during sexual excitement).

If the disease spreads further, to a woman's urethra and fallopian tubes, she may experience pain on one or both sides of the lower abdomen, vomiting, fever, or irregular periods. These symptoms are probably an indication of PID (see below). The fallopian tubes may become kinked and blocked, causing permanent sterility. Even a very young woman who gets this form of the disease would then never be able to have a child.

Both men and women can also get gonorrhea in the rectum, the throat, and the eye. That's because both the penis's and the vagina's discharge contains *gonococci* (the bacteria that spread gonorrhea) that can infect any warm, moist surface. If the discharge comes in contact with a person's rectum, for example, either by accident or through anal sex, the rectum becomes infected. Symptoms then include anal irritation, discharge, and painful bowel movements.

In the same way, if a person has oral sex with someone who has gonorrhea, the gonococci can infect the person's throat. Again, this may produce no immediate symptoms, or it may show up as sore throat or swollen glands.

Finally, if a person touches gonorrheal discharge and then touches an eye, the eye can also become infected.

Men can be tested for gonorrhea fairly easily; the doctor simply has to take a sample of the discharge and have it examined under a microscope. Sometimes a woman can be tested in that way, too, but it is only 50 percent accurate for women. As with most other aspects of gonorrhea, the situation is more difficult for a woman: a better test is for the doctor to take smears from inside her body (her urethra, upper vagina, and cervix) and wait two days to see if the smears produce cultures (cells grown in a laboratory) that reveal the presence of gonorrhea. A woman needs a follow-up test five to seven days after treatment, and a second test after her next menstrual period. A woman can't be treated while being tested, since the test won't be accurate, so some women prefer to be treated when their partners are being treated, just in case.

A woman who's going in to be tested for gonorrhea should make sure not to douche (to force a stream of water or other liquid into the vagina to clean it) just before the test. The douching might wash away some of the bacteria, making it seem that the woman has no disease when she really has.

A pregnant woman should be tested for gonorrhea at least once. That's because a pregnant woman with untreated gonorrhea might infect her baby as the baby passes through the birth canal. If the baby comes in contact with the gonococci as it is being born, it might go blind. However, all newborns are routinely given eyedrops to help prevent this, whether or not the mother has gonorrhea.

People who have gonorrhea must not have sex until the gonorrhea is cured, since their chances of infecting their partner are very high. They should avoid alcohol, which seems to encourage the disease. They should be careful to wash their hands with soap and water each time they urinate or move their bowels, drying them with a towel that nobody else uses.

Penicillin is the standard treatment for gonorrhea. Recently, however, there has been an upsurge of gonorrhea, particularly among young people and in the inner cities (see Chapter 3 for more details), and many of the latest outbreaks seem to be caused by a strain of the bacteria that resists penicillin. New treatments are being developed.

Generally, a person with gonorrhea may be fairly sure that the disease can be cured, particularly if it is caught in early stages. However, a woman may find herself permanently sterile as a result, and her chances of sterility go up each time she catches the disease.

Obviously, then, anyone who has gonorrhea must be sure to tell all of his or her sexual partners, or must ask the doctor or clinic to notify the partners (you can often have your partners told while keeping your own name out of it).

Using a condom for sex with men is a good general protection against gonorrhea from genital or anal sex. That's no protection for couples who practice fellatio (mouth-to-penis sex) or cunnilingus (mouth-to-women's-genitals sex). (Generally, being on the receiving end of oral sex is safe, but performing oral sex exposes you to a risk.) This is true whether or not the oral sex results in either partner coming— it's just a matter of the warm, moist mouth providing a "home" for the bacteria living in the discharge from a penis or vagina.

The best way to prevent gonorrhea is to be careful about whom you have sex with. As we have seen, genital, anal, and oral sex can all transmit gonorrhea, and both heterosexual and homosexual couples are vulnerable to this disease. The more partners you have, the greater chance you have of being exposed to gonorrhea. Even if you have only ever had sex with only one person, your chances of exposure go up if your partner has had a lot of partners.

Another good prevention for gonorrhea is to make sure that you can trust your partner, both to be honest with you about his or her symptoms, and to be careful enough to notice and check out any symptoms he or she may have.

You can also be watchful about your partner's body, noticing and asking about any unusual discharges.

Genital Warts

This disease is caused by a virus and can be cured by removing the warts; however, it is possible to carry the virus that causes genital warts—human papilloma virus, or HPV—and not have any symptoms. These symptom-free people can still infect others. Therefore, this disease is on the rise, and health officials estimate that two-thirds of the sex partners of people that have it will also get the disease.

As the name suggests, genital warts are hard, fleshy bumps in the genital area. They can also occur around the anus. In women, they can show up inside the vagina or on the cervix, which means that they might not be visible or even noticeable. They usually show up within three months of exposure.

Genital warts are the result of infection that enters the body through the penis, the urethra, the tissue around the anus, the vulva, the vagina, or the cervix. They are contracted during sexual intercourse or anal sex when the wart virus passes from one person's wart into the skin of the partner. There may be one wart or several; they may be visible or too tiny to see. Once warts are contracted, they tend to spread to other parts of the genitals.

The warts themselves are usually not dangerous. Doctors can get rid of them by freezing, burning, chemical solutions, or sometimes surgery. However, warts tend to come back in many of the people who have had them, either in the same place or in a different place. (The chance of recurrence depends on the locale where they first occurred: there is a 50 percent chance if the warts were on the vulva or vagina but only 5 percent if they were on the cervix.)

What makes genital warts dangerous is that some subtypes of virus that cause them may be linked with cancers of the penis, vulva, and cervix. Women who have been infected with genital warts should get twice-yearly Pap smears to make sure that any cancer is caught earlier, before it has time to develop. The best way to keep from getting genital warts is to use a condom. However, condoms don't prevent passsage of the virus from the scrotum to the vulva or visa-versa. But they can prevent internal warts in women and penile warts in men. Remember, you can't always see a person's warts, and your partner may not even know that he or she has them. If you have had sexual intercourse, you might want to ask your doctor to test you for genital warts at your next checkup, especially if you're a female.

Genital Herpes

This common STD—some 500,000 U.S. cases per year—is caused by a virus, known as *herpes simplex*. It takes the form of sores—like cold sores—in the genital area. The sores usually show up within 10 days of infection and heal within three weeks. After that, however, a person with herpes can experience a flare-up of the sores at any time.

The first attack of genital herpes is the worst. It usually follows sexual contact—either oral, anal, or genital—with a person who was recovering from a herpes attack. About five to seven days after the contact, a woman develops a small itchy area inside her labia major (outer lips), and a man develops a small itchy area on the shaft of his penis. Some people get headaches or fevers along with the attack; others just feel sick or as though they're getting the flu.

About 24 hours later, the itchy area develops small reddish bumps that turn into blisters by the next day. Generally, the area is tender and painful. A woman's labia may become so swollen that it hurts her to urinate.

Eventually, the blisters burst, leaving behind ulcers, or sores. The sores scab over in four or five days, and after a week or two has passed, they are usually completely healed. However, during the healing process and for about a week afterward, the virus is very easily spread from the infected area. If a person's mouth or genitals touch the infected areas, that person is likely to get herpes, too.

In most adults, herpes sores are more of an annoyance than a real danger. However, this disease can always be passed on to a partner, even when the sores are not visible or don't seem to be active. And since herpes can never be cured, the risk of passing this disease on to someone you are intimate with is always there.

Another danger with genital herpes sores is that they might be scratched with a hand that would then touch a person's eye, raising the possibility that the blisters and ulcers would seriously damage the eye. To prevent this, a person with herpes sores should wear underpants to bed, to prevent scratching the sores during sleep.

Some doctors prescribe medication to apply to the sores, to ease the itching. People should make sure to wash hands well after touching the infected area for any reason, even to apply medication.

When a person has herpes, some of the virus travels down the nerve that supplies the part of the skin that the virus has attacked. The virus travels until it reaches a larger, roundish part of the nerve, called a *ganglion*, near the *spinal cord* (the bundle of nerves that travels up the back). There it stays for the rest of the person's life. (If you have had chicken pox, that virus remains in your ganglion in the very same way.)

Sometimes the herpes virus stored in the ganglion is triggered to travel back to the area of the skin that was previously affected. No one knows why this happens. Some people believe it's related to stress, or to the menstrual cycle, but no studies have been able to document this. In any case, when the virus gets back into the skin, it might or might not cause a new attack.

The biggest danger associated with herpes is to unborn and newborn children of mothers with herpes. If a child is born while a mother's sores are active, the baby has a 50–50 chance of getting herpes. Two-thirds of the babies who get herpes at birth die; about half of the ones who survive suffer permanent brain or eye damage.

The drug *acyclovir* can be taken daily to help control herpes, but it is extremely expensive. Mothers with active herpes must have *Caesarean* deliveries—delivery by operation rather than giving birth vaginally. If there are no active lesions during pregnancy, then a vaginal delivery is safe.

If you or your partner is suffering from a herpes attack, you may be able to see it if you know what to look for. However, sores can also occur inside a woman where they are not visible and she is still infectious for the week after the sores heal—and may be infectious others times as well. Furthermore, a person might pass along the herpes virus unknowingly, without ever having had a serious enough herpes attack to even realize he or she has the virus. The best protection against getting herpes is to use a condom.

Pelvic Inflammatory Disease (PID)

The *pelvis* is the lower part of the body, the part that includes the internal and external sexual organs. Pelvic inflammatory disease affects only women, although they may get the disease as the result of infections or diseases that men have.

PID is actually not a single disease, but rather a complication that can result from other diseases, including sexually transmitted ones. In fact, PID is the most frequent complication that women experience from STDs. According to an October 1991 *Newsweek*, there are 420,000 cases of PID per year—plus many unreported cases.

The term *PID* means any kind of infection that gets into a woman's fallopian tubes, ovaries, uterus, or some combination of those organs. Because the kinds of organisms that can infect these parts of a woman's body are often passed through sex, PID is considered a sexually transmitted disease. What that means is that if a woman develops PID, she needs to make sure that her sexual partners are tested and treated for any conditions they may have that are infecting her.

When an infection spreads to the ovaries or fallopian tubes, it causes scars that may keep the ovaries from sending eggs into the fallopian tubes. Thus PID causes *infertility* (the inability to have children). It may also cause fertilized eggs to emplant in the walls of the fallopian tubes, rather than in the uterus. Since a baby cannot develop inside a fallopian tube, a so-called tubal, or ectopic, pregnancy results in the destruction of the *embryo* (the first form of an unborn child), as well as endangering the life of the mother. PID can also turn into *peritonitis,* a life-threatening type of infection. Sometimes PID causes infection in a woman's eyes or in the eyes of her newborn infant. Some types of PID infection raise the woman's chances of miscarriage, *stillbirth* (giving birth to a dead child), or early infant death.

The problem with PID is that it has so many different symptoms—and a woman might have some, all, or none of the symptoms before experiencing serious complications. Women who have had no idea that they were sick have suddenly found themselves in the hospital from the severe pain caused by a flare-up of PID. The following symptoms may or may not be experienced by a woman who is suffering from PID:

- lower abdominal pain
- sudden fever that come or goes
- swelling or tenderness in the cervix, uterus, or surrounding areas; swollen abdomen or lymph nodes (ask your doctor to show you how to check for swollen lymph nodes)
- pain around the kidneys or liver (in the lower back or lower stomach)
- increased menstrual cramps
- irregular bleeding or spotting
- increased pain during ovulation (which usually occurs 10–14 days before a menstrual period)
- unusual discharge from the vagina or urethra
- difficulties or a burning feeling when urinating
- lack of appetite; nausea or vomiting
- chills
- pain in the lower back or the legs

- acne-like rashes on the back, chest, neck, or face
- feeling weak, tired, depressed
- lowered interest in sexual activity

PID can be diagnosed by an examiner who finds lower abdominal pain or uterine or fallopian tube pain during a pelvic exam. Other primary symptoms are fever, an elevated white blood count, and cervical discharge. Sometimes, though, when PID has spread beyond the cervix, it can be diagnosed by *laparoscopy*, a hospital procedure in which the doctor makes a small slit below the navel and inserts a *scope* (a viewing device) into the *abdomen* (the belly). PID can also be diagnosed with an endometrial biopsy, an office procedure in which the doctor inserts a narrow device through the cervix into the uterus to obtain a small sample of endometrial tissue.

Most PID comes from infection caused by the same bacteria that cause STDs, especially gonorrhea and chlamydia. Almost all PID is experienced by women who have sex with men. A woman's male sexual partner might have no symptoms and yet infect her with organisms that cause PID.

A woman is most vulnerable to developing PID if she has sex during her period or during ovulation (which occurs during the two weeks or so before the period). That's because the cervix is more open during these times. So if bacteria attach themselves to moving sperm in the man's semen, they have an easier time getting into the areas that are dangerous for them to infect.

Women who use the birth-control pill seem to be less likely to get PID, since the pill seems to create a thick mucus in the cervix that keeps the sperm—and the bacteria-from entering. The best way to prevent PID, however, is for the man to wear a condom and for the woman to wear a diaphragm with *spermicide* (a jelly or cream that kills sperm to prevent pregnancy and that may also kill infectious organisms) during sex.

Ironically, *douching* (forcing a stream of water or other liquid up into the vagina to clean it) may increase the risk of PID, since it carries bacteria further up into the woman's organs. The vagina is a naturally self-cleaning organ, so women should not need to do more than wash regularly in order to stay clean and fresh. If a woman is concerned about a smell or discharge in the vaginal area, she should see a doctor about it rather than trying to douche it away, which may just make the problem worse.

The *IUD* (intrauterine device—a type of birth-control device that fits inside the uterus) might also increase the risk of PID by providing bacteria with a more open route into the uterus. If you have PID, you should use some other type of birth control. You should also avoid wearing tampons, which force bacteria upward into the uterus.

Various antibiotics can combat the condition. A woman who has gotten PID should make sure that her partner is tested and that she doesn't have intercourse with him until he too has completed treatment. It may be difficult to convince a man that he is part of the problem, especially if he himself doesn't have any symptoms, but if you have sex with a man who may have infected you, you are only making the problem worse.

Hepatitis

This virus may be transmitted in other ways, but sex is the leading mode of infection. There are two main varieties of this disease: hepatitis A, which is a relatively minor disease, and hepatitis B, which is far more serious. The CDC reports 300,000 cases of hepatitis B in the United States per year.

Hepatitis A is present in the *feces* (bowel movements) of a person who has the disease. If a person comes in contact with the infected feces and then with food (say, by not washing hands after going to the bathroom and then preparing food for someone else), he or she will infect the food. Another person who eats the food may then catch the disease. Hepatitis A can also be transmitted during sex, especially in sexual acts that involve either the mouth or the anus.

If a person catches hepatitis A, he or she will start to feel sick about 30 days after the infection. Adults then get *jaundice*—a condition that turns the eyes and the skin yellow. Children often don't have symptoms. Once either an adult or a child has gotten hepatitis A, the person develops *antibodies*, proteins that fight disease, that protects him or her from getting it again.

Hepatitis B, however, may not go away. A person who has had this more serious disease may continue to carry it, and to be able to infect others, especially if he or she has caught this disease early in life. As with hepatitis A, an infected person can infect another person through close contact, especially sexual contact involving the mouth or the anus.

The hepatitis B virus—or HBV—attacks the liver, causing an illness that acts something like the flu. Unlike the flu, however, the illness doesn't go away for a long time. It may also produce jaundice. Most people then go on to recover and to develop a natural immunity to the disease.

In some people, though, the virus takes root. It continues to be contagious, and it may lead to cirrhosis or cancer of the liver. Fortunately, there is a vaccine to protect against this disease, but many people who are at risk have not yet taken advantage of it.

The chances of getting hepatitis B go up as a person has more sexual partners. The chances of becoming a carrier also go up. Because of the way this disease is spread, men who practice anal sex with other men are most likely to get it, and the disease has been a somewhat serious problem in the gay male community.

As with other STDs, a condom offers some protection against hepatitis A and B. A person can get blood tests to find out whether he or she has been infected, is immune, and is a carrier. If a person is a carrier, he or she should make sure that all sexual partners have been given the hepatitis B vaccine.

Syphilis

This disease is far rarer than the other STDs discussed so far in this chapter—134,000 total U.S. cases of syphilis, with 50,00 U.S. cases of primary and secondary syphilis among 15–19-year-olds. However, like other sexually transmitted diseases, this one is on the rise. Syphilis is curable by penicillin if it is caught in time; if it is caught too late, the effects can be terrible, including blindness, insanity, and infecting, deforming, or killing an unborn fetus.

Syphilis spreads through open sores or rashes that contain the syphilis bacteria. The sores usually develop on the soft, mucous membranes of the genitals, mouth, and anus. However, a person may have syphilis sores on other parts of the body, and these are just as infectious as sores in the other three areas. A person may also get syphilis through broken skin on other parts of the body.

Syphilis spreads through the body extremely quickly. By the time symptoms develop, the infected person has already been affected by the disease. Within half an hour of being infected, the disease has spread to the lymph nodes in the genital area. Then they get into the bloodstream, which carries them into just about every part of the body. If the disease isn't treated, it gradually spreads to almost the whole body.

It takes about three weeks for a person to realize that he or she has syphilis. That's because it takes that long for the body to mobilize its defenses against the invading bacteria. The first sign of the disease is a raised pimple that appears on the vulva or the penis—a result of the body's sensitized blood cells attacking the syphilis. As the body continues to fight the disease, a hard tissue develops around the pimple. Eventually, blood supply to the pimple is cut off, so that the pimple's center dies and falls off, leaving an ulcer—a kind of open sore. Eventually, the ulcer heals, leaving as scar.

This entire process takes from three to eight weeks. However, the ulcer may be so small that it isn't noticed, so the infected person never seeks treatment. A person might also confuse it with other growths or pimples in the genital area.

A syphilis ulcer is very distinctive, however. It has firm edges and a soft center. Clear fluid comes out of the raw center of the ulcer. This fluid is infected, and if another person comes in contact with it, he or she can catch syphilis. This ulcer is known as a *chancre* (pronounced "shanker").

Generally, a person gets a chancre in the place where the syphilis entered his or her body. About 95 percent of the time, that's the genital area. Sometimes, though, it might be the fingertips, lips, breast, anus, or mouth.

As with gonorrhea, syphilis's initial symptom is much harder to detect in women than in men. A woman may have a syphilitic chancre on her cervix, deep inside her body, where neither she nor her partner can see it, but where it continues to threaten her with terrible disease as well as threatening to infect any partner. A woman may also get a chancre inside her vagina or in the folds of her labia, where she has difficulty seeing it. Thus only about 10 percent of women who get chancres notice them.

Ironically, although these symptoms are very mild, this is the time that the disease is most infectious. That means that the time that a person is most likely to give you a disease is precisely the time that he or she may not even realize that there is a disease. This is especially true because the sore disappears with or without treatment, usually in one to five weeks. Even though the sore is gone, the bacteria are still within in the body, spreading and multiplying.

This period of having a chancre is known as the *primary stage* of syphilis. The next stage is the *secondary stage*. This takes place a week to six months later, when the bacteria have spread all through the body. This stage usually lasts for weeks or months, although it might go on for years. Symptoms will come and go, and once again, they might be confused with something else, such as the flu.

Symptoms of the secondary stage include a rash on the entire body or on the palms of the hands and soles of the feet, a sore in the mouth, aching bones, swollen joints, a sore throat, a mild fever, or a headache. A person with syphilis might lose hair or discover a raised area around the genitals and anus. At this point, syphilitic sores may appear on any part of the body, so any kind of kissing or physical contact with bare skin can spread the disease. A doctor or clinic must give you a blood test specifically looking for syphilis to detect the disease at this stage.

The *tertiary* or third stage of syphilis is also known as the *latent* stage. Latent means "lying in wait," and it reflects the fact that at this stage, there are no symptoms. All the time, however, the disease is lying in wait, eating away at the heart, the brain, or other organs. This stage may go on from two to 20 years. After the first few years, it is not infectious. The only way you can tell whether you have syphilis at this stage is by having a blood test.

In some cases, syphilis stops at this stage. Although infected individuals don't go on to develop the truly frightening symptoms of late-stage syphilis, they do have a shortened life expectancy (that is, they tend to die earlier than they would if they hadn't caught syphilis). Generally, however, syphilis moves on to its final stage.

The symptoms of late-stage syphilis depend on which organs the syphilis bacteria have infected. A person might develop heart disease, blindness, mental incapacity (the result of an infected brain), crippling, or a combination of these symptoms.

Although this final stage of syphilis used to be relatively common among people who were infected, it is now much less so. That's because we can diagnose syphilis with a simple blood test, and treat it—at an early stage—with penicillin or other drugs. However, reported cases of syphilis have been going up since 1984, particularly in the inner cities. (For more details, see Chapter 3.) With the increase in this disease, there is also a greater chance of people allowing it to go untreated.

Sadly, syphilis can be passed on to unborn children through the mother's bloodstream. A child born with the disease is said to have *congenital* (from birth) syphilis. About

25 percent of infected fetuses die inside the mother's body. Another significant portion die early in life unless they are treated. Many of those that live develop signs of *tertiary*, or third—stage, syphilis between the ages of seven and 15.

A pregnant woman is usually routinely tested for syphilis, so that she and her child can be treated. Infants treated early can be cured. With the proper testing and treatment, no child needs to be born with congenital syphilis.

Syphilis can be diagnosed and treated at any time, by means of a simple blood test. However, since this disease has become relatively rare, doctors and other health workers might confuse the early stages of syphilis with some other STD.

If you've discovered a chancre or sore, be sure not to treat it with any kind of ointment or medication before a doctor or clinic worker has seen it. You should also make sure to get a blood test for syphilis. If you have been recently treated for gonorrhea with some medication other than penicillin, you should have four tests for syphilis, one month apart, to make sure that the syphilis—if there is any—is discovered in time for treatment.

Most people are treated for syphilis with some form of penicillin. After treatment, at least two follow-up blood tests are necessary—to make sure the disease is completely cured. People who have syphilis should not have any kind of sexual intercourse for a month after treatment ends.

Although the symptoms for syphilis make it sound like a frightening disease, it's good to remember that the first three stages are completely curable. Even the horrible symptoms of late-stage syphilis can be slowed or stopped. The key is not to be so afraid of finding out the truth that you avoid testing or treatment.

People have been known to get syphilis in ways other than having sex, but these cases are so rare they aren't worth mentioning. You can't get syphilis from using the same bathroom as an infected person, or from sharing food or utensils with him or her.

However, you can get syphilis from deep kissing someone, if he or she has a syphilis mouth sore. You can also get syphilis from oral or anal sex as well as from genital sex. If a person has a syphilis sore elsewhere on his or her body, such as on the finger or the breast, you can get syphilis from that sore coming in contact with your mouth, your genitals, your anus, or any broken places on your skin. That's because syphilis needs the warm, moist parts of the human body to survive.

Using a condom provides some protection. At least it will prevent a woman from being infected by a sore on the man's penis, or a man from being infected by a sore in the woman's vagina or rectum. A condom is no protection against mouth sores or sores on a person's fingertip or breast.

Therefore, the best way to prevent syphilis is, once again, to know your partner. "Knowing your partner" doesn't just mean knowing how many brothers or sisters your partner has, or knowing what his or her dreams are after high school. It means having an accurate idea of how many people your partner has slept with, whether a partner has ever been with a prostitute, and whether a partner will be honest enough to tell you if he or she notices sores or other symptoms. It means trusting your partner to be smart and self-protective enough to be aware of symptoms and to go to the doctor for tests and treatment. (For more on knowing a partner, see Chapter 5.)

AIDS

Acquired immune deficiency syndrome (AIDS) is probably the most publicized sexually transmitted disease these days. AIDS *is* an important disease, and a frightening one, so much so that we have devoted all of Chapter 4 to it. Yet you would do well to keep in mind that, numerically, it is the most rare of all the diseases that we have discussed in this chapter— 244,939 total AIDS U.S. cases as of December 1992. Make sure to understand and protect yourself against AIDS—but don't forget the other seven STDs, which are likely to be a more immediate threat to you.

You can find out a great deal more about AIDS in Chapter 4. Here, let us simply review the basic facts. AIDS comes from a virus known as the *human immunodeficiency virus,* of HIV. This virus can be *transmitted* (passed along) through either semen or blood and can only enter the body through the bloodstream. Possibly the virus can also be transmitted through other bodily fluids, such as vaginal fluids or the fluids that come out of a man's penis before orgasm. The virus is almost certainly not transmitted through tears, saliva, or sweat.

Anyone can get AIDS if he or she engages in certain high-risk behaviors: having unprotected sex with someone who is infected, sharing a needle with someone who is infected, getting a blood transfusion with contaminated blood. (AIDS can also be passed from a pregnant woman to her fetus.) You can't get AIDS from anyone in any other way, including a casual kiss on the cheek, sharing a bathroom, or eating together.

In the United States, AIDS has been most common among homosexual and bisexual men. A growing number of IV (intravenous) drug users (people who "shoot up") are also getting the disease. Women who have had sex with bisexuals, and the men and women who have had sex with IV drug users are increasingly getting the disease as well.

In heterosexual intercourse, it is far more common for men to give AIDS to women than the other way around. However, a woman who is having her period may transmit AIDS to her partner through her menstrual blood. Lesbian transmission of AIDS is virtually nonexistent.

People who have had sex with more than one person, or whose partners have had sex with more than one person, are at a higher risk of getting AIDS. So are people on the receiving end of anal sex. Cunnilingus (oral sex with a woman) is relatively less dangerous than either anal or vaginal sex, as long as the woman isn't having her period. Fellatio (oral sex with a man) is also relatively less dangerous, as long as the man doesn't come in the woman's mouth or near her vagina.

The best way to prevent AIDS is to abstain from sex. For people having sex with men the best way to prevent AIDS is to use a condom, and for people having sex with menstruating women to use a dental dam. It's also a good idea to ask your partner if he or she has ever been tested for AIDS, used IV drugs, or had more than two or three sexual partners. However, even a person who wants to be honest may be mistaken or forgetful about some dangerous part of his or her history. Communication is important, but it's no substitute for a condom.

You can find out whether you are HIV positive (have the AIDS virus in your body) by having a simple blood test. People who are HIV positive may or may not get AIDS (most do, but scientists are still learning about the disease). However, they can certainly infect other people. The incubation period for AIDS is up to 10 years, so a person might go on infecting people for years without even realizing it.

If both members in a couple have tested negative for HIV ("testing negative" means that there is no—negative—virus in the blood) and they go on to have sex only with each other for six months and do not share IV needles with anyone or have a blood transfusion, and then they both test negative again, most doctors agree that they can then stop using condoms (but should use some other form of birth control). However, if either person has sex with another person even once or has engaged in other high-risk behavior, he or she is putting the partner at risk. Rather than taking that risk, it's best to use a condom.

3

STDs Are on the Rise

A couple of nights before their "big date," Elise and Martin go to a movie together. The movie is about a teenaged couple in love who get married and have a baby. Afterward, they talk about the movie, and then, somehow, they start talking about themselves. Martin asks Elise if she ever wants to have children. Elise says she does, but not for years—there are lots of things she wants to do first. Martin says he feels the same way.

Elise takes a deep breath, gathers her courage, and says, "Well, maybe we should take precautions on Friday night then. Do you have something?" Martin says he doesn't. He's been thinking about it, but the whole idea of going into a drugstore to buy condoms makes him feel weird. Plus, since he's never used one, he isn't really sure how to put one on. It just seemed like one more thing that he might do wrong. He had been hoping that Elise was on the pill. Both of them realize that if they weren't talking about it now, they would just have done it on Friday, with Martin assuming that Elise was protected, and Elise hoping that she just wouldn't get pregnant somehow.

Then Martin says, "What about AIDS?" Elise says she heard that if you use a condom, you can't get AIDS. She also heard something about spermicide, but she isn't really sure what it is, how to get it, or how important it is.

Even though Richard seems to be freaking out, Charlie goes ahead and gets tested at the agency that he found out about on the hot line. They tell him that they'll let him know the results within a week. They also give him an hour's worth of counseling along with the test.

Charlie finds out that it's not true that you just "have to take the risk" if you want to have sex. There are some kinds of sexual contact that have no risk at all. Some other kinds of sex are somewhat risky, but if you know your partner well and take certain precautions, you can keep the risk down. Still other kinds of sex are very risky, even if you do take precautions. The counselor tells Charlie that everyone must decide for himself or herself what kinds of risks are OK and what kinds of risks are just not acceptable.

Charlie realizes that he and Richard have never talked about their past histories. He has never had any relationships before Richard, but he's pretty sure Richard is a lot more experienced than that. He has no idea if Richard was careful with his partners, or even if Richard's partners later came down with AIDS. Even though it's clear Richard doesn't want to talk about their relationship, Charlie knows that they have to talk.

Marisol tells Robert about PID. Robert is also afraid of going to his family doctor, so together they look in the yellow pages for a clinic to go to. They find one where people can get treated for free, and Robert goes to get examined for any infection that might be related to Marisol's PID. Luckily, he doesn't seem to have it, but he and Marisol realize they must make some decisions about their relationship. Are they going to be exclusive with each other? If not, what kind of precautions should they take, with each other and with the other people?

Robert and Marisol talk about these problems for a while, but they can't come to any conclusions. Even though right now neither of them is interested in anybody else, Robert says that sometimes he just likes to go off and be with someone "just a few times." He wants to keep this freedom— but he doesn't want to put Marisol—or himself—in any danger. Marisol would rather have an exclusive relationship, but she's willing to accept Robert's arrangements—except that she doesn't want to expose herself to any possible diseases from Robert's partners.

Getting Perspective

It may seem to you that you have been hearing an awful lot about STDs these days—at school, on television, perhaps at home. You might be wondering why. Are people just trying to scare you? Do they just want to frighten you away from sex with horror stories? After all, people have been having sex for a long time. Is it really possible that now, all of a sudden, it's so dangerous?

The answer to that question is yes. And no. Sexually transmitted diseases have a long history. They've probably existed for as long as human beings have had sex. But their history has been uneven, a kind of up and down movement between times when STDs have posed a serious threat to human life and health, and times when this problem has been less severe. After World War II, STDs became a far less severe problem in the United States because of the widespread use of antibiotics. Now, however, sexually transmitted diseases are on the rise in many frightening new ways. Diseases like gonorrhea that used to be curable are now sometimes resistant to traditional treatment. New diseases like AIDS and chlamydia have appeared, some of which are curable, some of which are not. And diseases that early testing and treatment had once virtually wiped out—gonorrhea and syphilis—are again on the rise.

To put this all in perspective, let's take a brief look at the history of sexually transmitted disease. Such diseases were once called "venereal diseases," ("VD" for short) after Venus, the Roman goddess of love. STDs go back even before Roman times, however. A disease that seems to be gonorrhea is even mentioned in the Bible. The Greek physician, Galen, gave that disease its name in 130 A.D. The ancient Greeks also wrote about the problem of genital warts.

By the 12th century in England, London brothel-keepers were forbidden by law from allowing clients to have sex with women who suffered from "the perilous infirmity of burning"—another reference to gonorrhea. The disease continued to spread throughout Europe and is frequently mentioned in literature of all types.

The Story of Syphilis

Some five years after Columbus returned from America, a new disease appeared in Europe—syphilis. The first description of the disease was noted by the Portuguese doctor Ruy Diaz de Isla, who worked in Barcelona, Spain. When he came to treat some of Columbus's men, he noticed a skin rash and ulcers in their mouths and throats. Within 15 years, the disease had spread throughout Europe.

Although some historians believe that syphilis simply did not exist in Europe until Columbus's men brought it back, others hold that the disease existed throughout Europe, Africa, and America, but that until 1494 or so, the symptoms were so mild that the illness had not been identified. Sometimes diseases change over time. In this view, syphilis suddenly went from being a mild disease to a very severe one.

In any case, as various armies traveled across Europe, they carried syphilis with them. Ironically, each country tried to blame its neighbor for the terrifying new sickness. The

Italians called it "the Spanish disease." The French, who were not infected until 1495, called it "the Italian disease" or "the Neapolitan disease" (the disease from Naples, a city in Italy).

Syphilis went on to infect people in Germany, Switzerland, Holland, and Greece by 1496. The following year it reached England, where, not surprisingly, it was called "the French disease." Scotland, Hungary, and Russia had seen the disease by 1500, when Vasco da Gama's Portuguese explorers were taking it to India. In 1505, the disease reached China. In 1506, it reached Japan, where it was called "manka bassam," or "the Portuguese disease."

Syphilis in those early days was a far more severe disease than it is today. The secondary stage was marked by ulcerated skin rashes (that is, skin rashes that were like open sores, releasing discharge), which were highly infectious even without sexual contact. According to current estimates, thousands of people seem to have died from this frightening disease, to such an extent that the Catholic church even appointed a patron saint to whom people with syphilis might pray.

Why did this early STD spread so quickly? There were several reasons:

1. No adequate method of testing and identifying the disease in its early stages existed. People didn't know they were infected—but they could still infect others.
2. No adequate means of preventing syphilis—while still having sexual contact—was available. Condoms and other modern preventive aids did not exist or were not effective.
3. People were not willing to modify their sexual behavior or to treat their partners with respect. Syphilis spread primarily through soldiers and sailors who visited prostitutes, who then infected local customers, who in turn went on to infect wives or other lovers. Soldiers and sailors might also have casual encounters with local

women or men, or they might simply rape the women, girls, or boys whom they encountered. A person who was frightened of an occupying soldier or a prostitute desperate to earn a living was not likely to find out whether her or his partner was infected. Women, girls, and boys might not have the choice of saying "no," even if they knew that a man was infected, let alone if they only suspected it or worried about it. Nor were lonely men in foreign countries who believed their only chance for sexual relationships was with prostitutes or casual encounters likely to be careful about their choice of sexual partner.

4. No effective treatment was available for syphilis in any of its stages. Once a person had the disease, he or she could continue to infect others, particularly through sexual contact with ignorant or desperate partners or with partners who didn't have the choice of saying no. Eventually, some hundred years later, the disease became far less severe and the pattern we know today developed. Over time, the disease became known as syphilis, after a poem written by an Italian doctor in 1530. The disease also became known as the "great pox" (as opposed to another disease, "smallpox"), which later became shortened to "the pox." (You can find several references to it in Shakespeare under this name.)

Even though the main way that syphilis spread was through prostitutes, no one was immune to it. As with STDs today, high-risk *behavior* was more important than high-risk *groups*. Even King Henry VIII of England was believed to have syphilis.

Syphilis became an unmentionable topic in the prudish atmosphere of the Victorian Era, during most of the 19th century in England. Even if people wouldn't talk about it, however, they still engaged in the behavior that spread it. In fact, it seemed that the more secretive and punishing people's attitudes were, the more quickly the disease spread. In the mid-19th century, soldiers in the United States, Britain, France, and Prussia (a part of today's Germany) were reported to have syphilis at the rate of 70 to 120 per 1,000. (That's 7 percent to 12 percent.) By the beginning of World War I in 1914, the rates had gone down to only about two-thirds of that amount. That seems to be because attitudes about sex had become more open, and the disease was no longer seen as a terrible punishment for an unforgivable sin. Widespread education, especially among poor and working people, also seems to have helped.

In fact, if we look at the decline of syphilis and gonorrhea between 1850 and 1910, we can see that it was almost entirely due to social factors: more open attitudes about sex, better health care for the poor, and improved public education. These dangerous STDs declined even though people still did not really know how to prevent them or to cure them.

Finally, in 1910, Dr. Paul Ehrlich, a German scientist, discovered salvarsan, the "magic bullet," which was able to cure syphilis. Meanwhile, the development of better microscopes had enabled doctors to identify the disease in its early stages, while a blood test invented by August von Wassermann made diagnosis possible even if there were no symptoms.

With early testing and treatment of syphilis available, you might think that the disease would have been virtually wiped out, or at least controlled, especially in industrialized countries with access to the latest health-care technology. Unfortunately, this has not been the case. Looking at the history of syphilis after the new medical discoveries were made is a sad lesson. It teaches us that even when a disease has become "unnecessary" because of new medication and scientific understanding, the disease may still persist because of poverty; lack of affordable health care; poor public education; negative attitudes toward sex, women, and homosexuals; and a host of other social factors.

Syphilis in the United States continued to be a problem for several decades. The disease had particular upsurges right after World War I and World War II, as a result of the increased number of soldiers in the population. It was generally more prevalent among poor people, whose poverty made them more likely to be prostitutes and to visit prostitutes. (The disease may have been more prevalent among upper-class people than statistics show, since they were more likely to be treated by private doctors who might not report the disease as readily as poor people's clinics.) Lack of education meant that a person might not know he or she had syphilis until it had reached an advanced stage. Lack of affordable health care meant that a person might not visit a doctor or clinic for testing or treatment. Both factors combined to make people less aware of how to prevent syphilis and other sexually transmitted diseases.

All of these social problems were compounded by racism, which produced segregated schools and health facilities. People of color, particularly African Americans, were far less likely to have the opportunity to get either a good education or adequate health care. The doctors they did see might not take their health problems as seriously, failing to offer proper health education or effective early treatment.

After World War II, this situation was changing. The disease had peaked at 76 per 100,000 after World War II. Then, improvements in income, health care, and education, plus the ending of the war and the return of soldiers to civilian life, where they were far less likely to visit prostitutes, all combined to reduce the incidence of syphilis to a low of only four people per 100,000 from 1955 to 1958. This figure is testimony to how well STDs *can* be controlled, if a society is committed to doing so.

In 1958, however, the trend began to reverse, and by 1965, the figure had gone up to 12 per 100,000—fully three times greater than it had been just 10 years earlier. According to Drs. Sevgi O. Aral and King K. Holmes, writing in *Scientific American*, this increase may have been the result of a decline in federal funding for syphilis control.

The story of syphilis continues to reflect changing social patterns. From 1965 to 1982, the rate stayed fairly constant among women but went up quickly among men, because of an epidemic among gay men. Those decades were the beginning of the gay liberation movement, during which homosexual men had new opportunities to increase their sexual activity, often in a culture of drinking, drugs, and casual sex. Sexually transmitted diseases flourish in such an atmosphere. First, increasing the number of sexual partners increases a person's risk of exposure to a disease. Second, having sex while drunk or high means that a person is far less likely to find out about his or her partner's health or past sexual history. Third, for both reasons, an infected person is very unlikely to inform all of his or her partners if an STD *is* discovered. That means that all the infected partners can continue to spread the disease without realizing that they or *their* partners are at risk.

From 1982 to 1986, the rate of syphilis among gay men dropped sharply. The AIDS epidemic had made it extremely clear to that community how important it was to know one's partner and to treat him responsibly.

In 1986, however, the syphilis rate began rising again, this time for both men and women. The majority of this figure seems to be the result of increasing prostitution among people addicted to crack and other drugs. In fact, within the "crack culture," people were frequently exchanging sex for drugs. Once again, STDs were passed on in an atmosphere in which people were not treating either themselves or their partners responsibly. Addicts' desperation was so great, their judgment so faulty, and their lack of access to health care and education so severe that they were becoming part of an epidemic that, from a medical standpoint, was totally unnecessary and preventable.

STDs Today

Gonorrhea has also increased sharply in the past few years, and for the same reasons that syphilis has. Although gonorrhea has declined overall since 1975, it has risen sharply since 1984 among African Americans. These statistics may be partly the result of white people being more likely to see private doctors, who are less likely to report gonorrhea in their patients. It seems clear, however, that the new connection of prostitution and illegal drug use is closely linked to the epidemic rise of gonorrhea.

New STDs

Besides new increases in these old STDs, recent years have seen the appearance of new STDs. The best-known, of course, is AIDS, which first came to national attention in 1981 when half a dozen cases were reported in Los Angeles. The Centers for Disease Control reported almost 250,000 cases in the United States—244,939 people actually have AIDS but 1.5 million are HIV positive.

Worldwide, the AIDS epidemic is growing at an even more alarming rate. In Africa alone, some 550 to 1,000 cases per every million adults are reported each year, according to John Langone's book *AIDS: The Facts*. According to *Newsweek*, the U.S. death rolls for AIDS totaled 120,000 by October 1991—more than the Vietnam War and the Korean War combined. The problem was expected to get worse, as more Americans died of AIDS in 1992 and 1993. (For more about AIDS, see Chapter 4.)

Chlamydia is another recent STD. It seems to have appeared in the past 25 years, although possibly it previously existed in such a mild form that it was barely noticed. The development of pelvic inflammatory disease (PID) from a variety of sources is also a fairly new phenomenon. According to a December 1991 issue of *Newsweek*, some 420,000 cases of PID are treated annually in the United States, while there are four million U.S. cases of chlamydia a year.

Like gonorrhea, PID seems to be declining. The 1992 annual report of the Centers for Disease Control showed that between 1982 and 1990, the disease dropped sharply—

probably because of increased awareness about sexual health and responsibility resulting from the AIDS epidemic. Nevertheless, according to the National Disease and Therapeutic Index nearly 11 percent of the nation's childbearing women are affected by PID, which, as we have seen, threatens them with sterility. Like most STD statistics, the figures have a racial component: one in 10 childbearing white women are affected, as compared to one in six childbearing African-American women. The discrepancy, once again, probably has to do with the differing standards of health care and education available to the two groups.

What Are Your Chances?

How likely are you to get a sexually transmitted disease?

Personal Choices

In one sense, the answer to that question is entirely up to you. Whether you choose to have sex (or various kinds of sexual contact), whom you choose to have a romantic relationship with, whether you use effective protection, whether you use good judgment in choosing a partner and ask him or her the relevant questions—all these matters are completely within your personal control. You might think of that as the "good news" about STDs—that you *can* take care of yourself by making good choices.

If you are going to have sexual relationships with men—including anal and oral sex—the best thing you can do is to use a condom. Anal sex without a condom is probably the most likely to transmit disease. Fellatio and cunnilingus seem to be the least risky forms of sex, as long as the man who is receiving fellatio doesn't come without a condom, and as long as the woman who is receiving cunnilingus doesn't have her period without using a dental dam. (For more on how to protect yourself within a sexual relationship, see Chapters 5 and 6.)

You should also be aware that gonorrhea is highly contagious. It is very easy to catch gonorrhea from someone after having sex with him or her only one time. Since there is now a new epidemic of gonorrhea especially among African-American inner-city teenagers, this is a disease to take seriously, even though it is receiving less publicity than AIDS.

Syphilis is likewise highly contagious during its early stages. Although it is far less widespread than gonorrhea, it is becoming increasingly frequent among crack users and among members of the drug culture in general, so if your partner has ties to that world, it makes sense to be especially cautious.

AIDS is somewhat less contagious than syphilis or gonorrhea. That is, it is somewhat less likely that you can catch AIDS from someone after having sex with him or her only once. Men are more likely to transmit AIDS to women (or to other men) than women are to transmit it to men. (For more details about AIDS, see Chapter 4.) However, it is certainly *possible* to catch the AIDS virus from someone after only one sexual encounter, and there have been many recorded examples of such infections.

Chlamydia and other infections leading to PID seem to be highly contagious. They are also the most widespread form of STD in the United States today, and they know no bounds of class or race. Although the diseases themselves are rarely fatal, they have a large chance of leading to sterility.

The Big Picture

A huge percentage of STDs in the United States are suffered by young people—many of whom are teenagers. According to *Newsweek*, some 12 million Americans get some kind of STD each year—and three million of those Americans are teenagers. That means some 25 percent of STD cases each year involve teenagers. Some 63 percent of U.S. STD cases involve people under 25.

These figures are especially sad because sterility in women so often results from STDs. Young women just starting out in their first relationships may be condemning themselves to a future where they can't even think about having children.

Clearly, if so many teenagers are contracting STDs, many teenagers must be sexually active. Many—but not all. By age 15, according to a study cited by Peggy Clarke, executive director of the American Social Health Association, some 27 percent of all American girls and 33 percent of all American boys have had sexual intercourse.

That's a large number, but it isn't everyone or even a majority. The numbers go up with age, but only to some extent. According to several studies done by the Centers for Disease Control, California State University, The University of California, and the U.S. Food and Drug Administration, about 57 percent of all high school students have had sex. But only 26 percent of the sexually active seniors surveyed said they always used condoms—even though condoms cut the risk of AIDS by 90 percent and have a similar preventive effect on other STDs.

Yet older students may be even less likely to use condoms. According to a study of California college students by sociologists Janice Baldwin and John Baldwin, less than 20 percent of all sexually active students use condoms 75 percent of the time or more. The Baldwins found that the people who were taking the most risks—having sex with the most partners or on the shortest acquaintance—were using the fewest precautions.

Many young people believe they don't need to use condoms because they love or trust their partners. They might be surprised to know that 34 percent of the college men in one study said that they lied in order to have sex. In a study of southern California college students, nearly half of the men and two-fifths of the women said they would lie about how many other people they had slept with. One man in five said he would lie about whether he had been tested for AIDS.

How common are STDs? Here is a chart showing the number of cases in the United States per year for the eight most common STDs:

1. Chlamydia—4,000,000 cases per year
2. Gonorrhea—1,300,000 cases per year
3. Genital Warts—1,000,000 cases per year
4. Genital Herpes—500,000 cases per year
5. PID—420,000 cases treated per year (There may be more untreated cases.)
6. Hepatitis B—300,000 cases per year
7. Syphilis—134,000 cases per year
8. AIDS—242,146 total AIDS cases through October 1992; 1.5 million HIV positive.

According to Derek Llewellyn-Jones, author of *Sexually Transmitted Diseases*, some 20 percent of the PID cases that women contract lead to permanent damage of the fallopian tubes. The milder infections may not block or prevent pregnancy, but if a woman has been infected and later becomes pregnant, she is four times as likely to have an ectopic pregnancy, in which the fertilized egg lodges in the fallopian tube rather than in the uterus. An ectopic, or "tubal," pregnancy is marked by internal bleeding, which causes severe pain. It usually requires surgery to save the life of the mother and always results in the death of the embryo. In the United States, the number of ectopic pregnancies increased from only 15,000 in 1984 to more than 75,000 in 1989, with many of these cases related to PID.

Who Is Responsible?

Personal Responsibility

In one sense, we can relate the rising epidemic of STDs to individual responsibility—to the choices that people make about whether, when, how, and with whom to have sex.

Certainly this is the part of the problem over which you have the most personal control. Taking responsibility may be difficult, frightening, or upsetting, and many people simply don't do it. They decide not to decide, believing that if they don't think about anything bad, it won't happen.

Of course, this doesn't work. In one study, one-third of men infected with HIV (the virus that leads to AIDS) and one-half of the HIV-infected women did not acknowledge any previous high-risk behavior. Whether they were lying, had forgotten, or genuinely didn't see their behavior as risky, they were clearly not reliable guides to their own level of risk—or to their partner's.

This wish to ignore the consequences of behavior doesn't just relate to STDs. It relates to other possible consequences of sexual relationships, like pregnancy. According to Michael Burnhill, associate professor of obstetrics (the field of caring for pregnant women and delivering babies) at the Robert Wood Johnson Medical School in New Jersey, 60 percent of *all teenagers* who are sexually active don't use birth control. Rather, they wait nine to 12 months after their first sexually transmitted disease experience to go to a clinic to get prescription *contraceptives* (birth control). Adults don't do much better, according to Burnhill—25 percent of them never use any birth control either.

Social Responsibility

But sexually transmitted diseases are not just a personal responsibility. They are also society's responsibility. The attitudes that society promotes about sex, teenagers, health, and disease clearly affect the climate in which you and other teenagers make your decisions. So do more concrete things, like the availability of STD clinics and birth-control clinics, and the availability of health care in general.

In this regard, the United States falls far behind other industrialized countries. According to Burnhill, "teen-agers in the United States have less sex, get pregnant more often, and have abortions more frequently than do teen-agers in any other civilized country." (Burnhill seems to be using the word *civilized* to mean *industrialized,* which may be an insulting choice of phrase—but his point is clear.) If a problem is so widespread throughout a country, and so different from other comparable countries, the problem can't just be individual. What is it about American values that would lead teenagers here to have sex *less* often and yet to get pregnant *more* often?

One reason might be the lack of available birth-control clinics and counseling. With the exception of South Africa, the United States is the only industrialized country in the world without some kind of national health-care system (a service that provides everyone basic health services free or at an affordable cost). The United States' provision of basic birth-control information and services is clearly far worse than that of other industrialized countries.

This problem of the government's role is certainly central to the question of STDs. In 1992, the National Institutes of Health spent $79 million on STD research and $1.3 billion to respond to AIDS. In 1993, the Centers for Disease Control spent $89 million on STD research and $504 million on AIDS research. Yet many experts have said that far more needs to be spent on treatment and education as well as research.

The U.S. government does currently fund some STD clinics, but these services are overwhelmed by the number of people who need help. According to Aral and Holmes, "STD clinics are closing earlier in the day, patients are waiting longer hours to receive care and greater numbers of people are being turned away without receiving care. Although people are invited to return the next day or after the weekend, the close association of STD with drug use and with sex for drugs ensures that many potential patients will continue to spread infection after being turned away." Aral and Homes go on to share the results of a study they conducted in May 1989, when they discovered that 19 of 23 public STD clinics in the United States reported one or more ways of delaying treatment. Like many others, Aral and Holmes believe that until government funding for STD clinics increases, and until STD facilities are expanded and improved, the problem of STDs will continue to get worse. They write, "In the 1990s, the solution to the STD crisis cannot rest solely on preventing high-risk behaviors in individuals."

Mixed Messages

What about the other part of Burnhill's point—that U.S. teenagers have sex less often but get pregnant more often then their counterparts in Europe, Japan, and South Africa? The combination of U.S. teenagers having sex less often yet getting pregnant more often suggests that something in the sexual attitudes of this country makes it difficult for teenagers to handle their sexuality honestly and responsibly.

Sexual desire for another person is one of the most powerful of all human feelings. The sense of wanting to be physically close to another, to touch and kiss the person and have that person touch and kiss you, is an emotion that is unique to human beings, who are capable of sexual response and sexual activity at any time after they mature physically.

Unlike animals, then, human beings get to decide when, how, and whether they want to have sex. Humans do seem to have cycles that might affect when they are feeling more or less sexual, all other things being equal—but if you're a human being, all other things are rarely equal! Being with someone whom you find boring might turn you off, even during a particularly sexual time. Hearing your favorite song with someone you like might turn you on, even during a less sexual time.

Also, unlike animal sexuality, human sexuality involves the mind as well as the body. The idea of another person might be almost as exciting as the actual person. Human beings can watch movies, read books, or look at pictures that are sexually exciting. We can have fantasies about how wonderful it would be to touch, kiss, or have sex with a person, fantasies that can produce sexual responses as powerful as an actual encounter. We can also have sexual responses to the parts or qualities of a person that aren't directly sexual. Hearing the voice of someone you love may be exciting, even if the person is only saying, "How do we get to Market Street?" Learning about a beloved person's good deed, sports triumph, or sad mood might fill us with feelings of love and tenderness.

Because human beings have such a wide range of choices and responses where sex is concerned, sexual feelings have been a complicated subject for all human beings in all societies, and each society has struggled to find its own way of dealing with them and understanding them. Are they just an "animal" response, part of our biological need to have children to continue the species? Are they part of a "higher" feeling called "love"? Are there "good" kinds of sexual responses along with "bad" ones? Is sexual feeling a sin that only marriage can make okay, or a low feeling that only love can turn into a higher emotion? Or is all sexual expression good for its own sake? Is it all right to have sexual feelings for someone of the same sex? For someone who is married or committed to someone else? For someone who doesn't have the same feelings toward you?

These are tough questions. If you've ever read any novels or poetry from another society or another period, you know that these have been tough questions throughout human history. Different religions, societies, and communities have developed their own rules for dealing with acceptable and unacceptable sexual behavior.

Currently, in the United States, we have many people from many different religions, cultures, and family traditions. We also have people from different generations, who may have grown up at a time when sexual practices and customs were different from what they are today. This mix of cultures and traditions can lead to confusion, where the rules you learn at home don't seem to fit with the way "everybody else" seems to be acting at school.

The confusion is made even greater by the mixed messages given by advertising, music, television, and the movies. In some cases, sex is portrayed as uplifting and all-involving. If a man loves a woman, his sexual desire for her might be shown as helping him to "reform," to find new courage, or to take some other important step in his life. If a woman loves a man, her sexual desire for him might be shown as inspiring her in a similar way, or as leading her to devote her life to him forever. People can see sex as part of true love and having sexual feelings for a person as a kind of guarantee that the two of you will be together forever.

On the other hand, sex is frequently portrayed as casual, trouble-free, and simply "fun." Both in commercials and in more developed stories, we often see images of a handsome man surrounded by a group of adoring women in bikinis, or a beautiful woman who catches every man's eye as she walks down the street. The sexual feelings portrayed in these images don't have anything to do with "forever" or "true love." But they do make sex seem easy and playful, with no serious consequences, either physical or emotional.

There is a third cultural attitude toward sex in America, one that says that sex is not something to show or talk about openly. In European television, for example, it has long been possible to show a woman's bare breasts or to portray a couple making love. European books and films have generally been more open about both sexuality in general and homosexual relationships than American books and movies. The popular television show *Beverly Hills 90210* caught something of this contradiction in one of its early episodes. The sophisticated students at the wealthy high school knew all about sex, birth control, even abortion. Yet they were required to get their parents' signatures before they were allowed to take a two-week sex education course, including hearing a speech by a young woman who had contracted AIDS.

As you go on to define your own sexual feelings, you might find these mixed messages confusing and upsetting.

Do sexual feelings guarantee true love, or are they just a way to have fun? Are there consequences to sex, and if so, what are they? Is it possible to have sex with one person and feel one way about it, and then to have sex with another person and have quite different feelings? Are all of your sexual feelings OK, or are some of them bad?

It might be helpful to remember that there are no simple answers to any of these questions. In other societies, the messages and rules about sex might be more consistent and clear. The good part of that would be the sense of protection and support that you might feel. The bad part would be the lack of choice. In our own society, the good part of all the confusion is that it gives you a chance to decide for yourself what kinds of sexual experiences are right for you. The bad part is that you might feel alone, confused, frightened, upset, or anxious as you try to work out your own standards and ideas.

Like it or not, sexual standards in the United States *are* confused, and teenagers today have to make their own decisions about how to handle this situation. Even if your parents have given you very clear instructions, and even if you decide to follow those instructions to the letter, you'll still come in contact with lots of people who aren't acting in that way, and you'll still have to decide if you want to follow your family's rules and not theirs.

What we can offer, though, are two facts that are always important to remember when dealing with sexual relationships:

Number one, sex always has consequences. In this way, it's just like any other biological activity. If you eat a candy bar, you might enjoy yourself—and you might gain weight. If you eat a bowl of cottage cheese, you might gain energy and nourishment—and you might be bored. If you eat a delicious steak dinner, you might both enjoy yourself and gain energy—or you might be one of those people who has a hard time digesting red meat.

Sex also has consequences, both physical and emotional. The physical consequences include possible pregnancy or disease, so you should make sure to take precautions against those possibilities if you decide to have sex.

Sex might also lead to strong emotions—your own, your partner's, or both. It almost always changes a relationship in ways you can't predict, perhaps making it closer, perhaps setting up expectations that one or both of you can't fulfill, perhaps making you feel more comfortable together, perhaps making you feel less so. Being ready to accept these consequences and learning about what kinds of feelings sex produces in you are part of growing up and making adult decisions.

Number two, sex with another person always involves another person's feelings and physical safety as well as your own. So by definition, you have a responsibility to your partner as well as yourself: to be honest, to respect the other person's feelings, and to make sure that neither of you suffers any unwanted physical consequences, like pregnancy or disease. If you can tell that you would take having sex with a person very seriously, but that the person in question might treat it more casually—or vice versa—you might want to think twice before getting involved. It's not fair for either of you to ask a partner to share your attitudes and ideas; it's not respectful of yourself to deny all your own feelings in favor of your partner's. And of course, it's never OK to force someone into doing something he or she doesn't want to do or to lie to someone to get what you want.

Part of the reason that sexually transmitted diseases are on the rise in America today is because, although teenagers are having sex at younger and younger ages, they don't find it very easy to talk about sex or to think about it rationally. That's not surprising; human beings have always had a hard time being rational about sex. And, as we have seen, a number of social factors, such as lack of health care and education, are part of the problem as well. At the same time, every person can make his or her own decisions about how to handle sexual relationships.

Knowing about STDs can be one important factor in those decisions, so that you can treat both yourself and your partner with caring and respect.

4

AIDS

Elise and Martin know they want to go ahead and make love together, but they decide that they have to make some decisions together, too. Since they both don't want to have children or to take chances with STDs, they decide that they should both do something about it. Martin goes to a drugstore in a different neighborhood and buys some condoms. He buys enough so that he can experiment by himself, ahead of time, with putting them on. At least he won't have to be nervous about that!

Elise also goes to a drugstore and asks the woman behind the counter about spermicide. The woman is very helpful and explains that Elise should look for foam that has non-oxynol-9 in it. There are other kinds of spermicide that she could use with a diaphragm, but to use with condoms, she should buy foam. Elise also practices putting the foam in ahead of time, so she doesn't have to worry either.

Martin and Elise feel like they're in love, but they can't quite imagine that neither of them will ever be interested in anybody else. Elise says that if Martin does something with some other girl just once, she probably doesn't even want to hear about it. But she also doesn't want to be in danger. Martin says he feels the same way. They agree that if either one of them ever has sex with anyone else, he or she will make sure to use condoms and foam with that person too. They also promise to be completely honest if either one thinks he or she has any symptoms of STDs, so that both of them could get tested and treated right away.

Even though it's hard talking about these things together, both Martin and Elise feel closer after they've done it. In a funny way, it's made them less nervous—after all, if they can trust each other to talk about these things, they can trust each other to be patient and caring even if each of them is clumsy or inexperienced.

Richard has been so upset at the idea of Charlie getting tested, even though Charlie's test was negative, that the two of them haven't seen each other for a few weeks. Finally, though, Richard calls and agrees to get together for a talk. He says he misses Charlie, and Charlie says he misses him, too.

When they meet, Charlie explains that he really cares about Richard, and he wants the two of them to stay together. But he also needs to know about Richard's sexual history, and he needs to know that anything they do together is going to be reasonably safe. Even though it's hard for Richard to talk about sex or about his other relationships, he realizes that's important to Charlie—and to him, too.

Richard tells Charlie that he used to hang out in a gay bar and pick up other guys to go home with. Charlie is his first real relationship, but he has been with several other guys. Since he didn't really know any of them, he doesn't know how big the risks were. He listens to Charlie describe his own experience of getting tested for AIDS and agrees that he'll get tested, too. That way, he and Charlie will know what they're dealing with.

When Richard's test comes back negative (meaning that he doesn't have any evidence of having the virus that causes

AIDS), he and Charlie are really relieved. But even though neither of them is infected now, they both know that it could happen to either of them. Slowly, they start talking about what kinds of precautions they want to take and what the rules of their relationship will be.

Marisol and Robert decide that they can't agree on what they both want. It's really important to Robert to have the freedom to see someone else besides Marisol occasionally. It's really important to Marisol to know that she and Robert have an exclusive relationship, both for emotional reasons and because Marisol doesn't want to be exposed to disease because of something Robert did with someone she doesn't even know. The two of them still care about each other, but if they can't agree, they're afraid they're going to have to break up.

Why Should You Stay Informed?

This chapter concerns AIDS, one of the fastest-growing sexually transmitted diseases in the United States and the world. In the following pages, we'll talk about what AIDS is, who gets it, and how to prevent it.

You should be aware, though, that our knowledge about AIDS is both incomplete and is changing rapidly. With a disease as widespread and as fast-changing as AIDS, it's important to stay informed. If they were doing construction work in your city or town, you'd be aware that any time you wanted to take a drive, you might have to check where the latest construction was in progress. That knowledge might affect the route you'd choose, the detours you'd plan for, and how quickly you could expect to get where you want to go. FInding out about AIDS—especially if you are or are planning to be sexually active—is a lot like that. You need to know the latest information so that you can make the best decisions, the ones that will make you feel most comfortable and keep you the safest.

What Is AIDS?

AIDS stands for "acquired immune deficiency syndrome." It is the name for a *syndrome* (cluster or pattern of diseases) that come from a *deficiency* (lack) in a person's *immune* system (the system that helps defend us from illness). When a person's immune system has been weakened or destroyed by AIDS, the person is vulnerable to many diseases that the body would ordinarily be able to fight off. Sometimes the person with AIDS (PWA) also gets diseases that others might also get, but gets them in a more severe form than others do. Eventually, a disease or combination of diseases becomes so severe that the PWA dies. AIDS itself doesn't kill; it simply opens the door to diseases that do.

AIDS is actually the final stage of a disease that starts with being infected by HIV—the human immuno-deficiency virus. Even though HIV is also sometimes called "the AIDS virus," when a person is first infected he or she doesn't actually have AIDS yet. Once a person is infected with this virus, it lies dormant in the body for weeks, months, or even years, sometimes as many as 10 years before any symptoms of disease are seen. Some researchers believe that a person with HIV in his or her blood has only a 20 percent to 50 percent chance of eventually getting AIDS. Others believe that people with HIV infection have a 100 percent of getting AIDS, sooner or later. This is just one of the areas where our knowledge is still incomplete and changing rapidly.

Currently, an estimated 1.5 million Americans have been infected with HIV—although some contend that this figure has been underestimated by as much as a half. Worldwide, as many as 13 million people might be infected with HIV according to the CDC's December 1992 statistics. Of these people the CDC estimates 611,589 have AIDS. Many of those who are HIV positive but who do not have AIDS are leading apparently healthy lives, with no visible symptoms or difficulties. However, each of them is capable of infecting someone else with HIV.

It's important to understand the difference between "having AIDS" and being infected with HIV. A person who has AIDS is very sick. A person who has been infected with HIV may have no visible symptoms. Either person could infect someone else, however, through sexual contact, sharing a needle, or having a baby. Neither person could infect someone else through casual contact, such as by sharing food or by a kiss on the cheek.

What Are the Symptoms of AIDS?

The First Stage

AIDS is the third stage of a three-stage progression. The first stage of this disease is infection with HIV. This stage has no symptoms. About two to eight weeks after exposure, a person who has been infected with HIV usually starts manufacturing *antibodies*, the body's natural defense against a virus or other type of infection. Sometimes, however, it takes up to six months for the antibodies to appear in a person's bloodstream.

When a person gets a blood test to find out if he or she has HIV, it's these antibodies that the test is looking for. That's why you can't be absolutely sure of an AIDS test unless you either haven't been having any kind of sex or using IV drugs for six months, or unless you and your partner have sex only with each other and haven't used IV drugs and then take the test again six months later. Otherwise, the test might just miss the antibodies that showed up in your blood after your latest sexual encounter.

The Second Stage

The second stage is ARC, or AIDS related complex. This stage is very poorly defined, but it appears to be a period of milder symptoms that might appear and disappear before AIDS itself sets in. These symptoms are not in themselves life-threatening. They also might result from other conditions, such as a bad cold, flu, or other type of illness. They include the following:

- swollen glands in the neck, armpits, or groin, with or without pain
- loss of appetite, or the unexplained loss of 10 pounds or more in less than two months
- weakness in the legs, especially climbing stairs
- night sweats, waking up drenched several nights in a row
- a fever that lasts more than a week
- chronic or long-lasting diarrhea
- a dry cough that doesn't come from smoking, a cold, or the flu
- white spots or blemishes in the mouth, whether painful or not (also known as oral thrush or candidiasis)
- white sores or thickening in the mucous membranes of the mouth, tongue, or vagina
- shingles-a kind of red blisters
- lymphoma—a cancer of the lymphatic system

The Final Stage

The last stage of the disease is AIDS itself. In this stage, which can occur as many as 10 years after the initial infection, a person is vulnerable to a number of painful or deadly diseases: forms of pneumonia and tuberculosis; painful herpes sores; Kaposi's sarcoma (a kind of cancer); dementia (a loss of mental abilities, sometimes accompanied by paranoia or wild mood swings); emaciation (severe loss of weight); along with a variety of rare diseases whose symptoms include headaches, fever, blindness or blurred vision, nausea, colitis (pains in the stomach or intestines), esophagitis (sores and pains in the throat), diarrhea, and lung problems.

Sometimes a person will die from AIDS very quickly. Other times, a person will get one or more of the AIDS-related diseases, seem to have recovered, and fall ill again. So far, there is no cure for AIDS and no vaccine that will prevent it, although some drugs, notably AZT, do seem to slow it down.

How Contagious Is AIDS?

In order to answer this question, we must first define the difference between *infectious* and *contagious*. An *infectious* disease is a disease that causes an infection. A contagious disease is a disease that can be spread from person to person. Malaria and measles are both infectious diseases: both of them infect human beings and cause certain symptoms. However, measles is highly contagious—it can be passed on by coughing or sneezing, can be picked up from someone's plate or dirty tissues, travels through air, food, and water. Malaria, on the other hand, is transmitted through mosquitos. A nurse taking care of a measles patient has to take precautions not to catch the disease (unless she or he is already immune); a nurse taking care of a malaria patient does not need to take any special precautions.

AIDS is contagious only under certain circumstances. The HIV that causes AIDS does not travel through food, air, or water. Thus kissing a PWA on the cheek, eating food he or she has prepared, sharing a bathroom with the person, even using the same toothbrush won't expose you to AIDS. The only way you can become infected with HIV from a person with AIDS or a person who is HIV positive is to share a needle or blood with the person or to have sex with him or her (or to be born to a mother with AIDS).

Here are a list of other ways that people have *not* been known to be infected with HIV:

- from a person's coughing or sneezing
- from contact with the person's tears, sweat, or saliva
- from body-to-body contact; e.g., a hug when both people are fully clothed, holding hands, giving a massage on bare skin.

Apparently, large amounts of the HIV are needed in order to be able to pass the virus on. The bacteria that causes hepatitis B, whose consequences are far less deadly, is actually far easier to pass on than the HIV. Health care workers have a 6 percent to 30 percent chance of getting hepatitis from accidental injuries with patients' hypodermic needles; they have less than a 1 percent chance of being infected with HIV that way, according to the Centers for Disease Control.

AIDS is a tragic disease that deserves national attention and allocation of resources. But it's important to remember that, in its first decade, 1981–91, it directly reached only about 1 percent of the U.S. population, killing a total of 171,890 Americans by December 1992, according to the CDC's February 1993 report. Cancer, by comparison, kills 472,000 Americans every year, while measles—a totally curable disease when the right care is available—kills some two million children a year in Africa and Latin America. Some scientists have commented that if AIDS were as contagious as many people imagine, no one in the United States would be left alive by now.

We mention these comparisons not to minimize the importance of AIDS, but to help us all keep a sense of proportion. It's important not to let the frightening rhetoric about AIDS paralyze us. It's important to prevent such incidents as the ones in Queens, New York, and Kokomo, Indiana, when schoolchildren with AIDS were kept from attending public school, or the numerous incidents taking place all over the

United States, of people with AIDS being fired from their jobs because their coworkers are afraid of this "mysterious" disease.

At the same time, it's important to remember that AIDS *is* contagious under certain circumstances, such as while having sex or while injecting drugs with a shared needle. You might think of AIDS' risks as a continuum, where one end is crossing in traffic with the light and the other end is running out onto a crowded freeway late at night in the rain. Clearly, one type of activity is far riskier than the other. Just as clearly, you wouldn't shut your eyes or read a book while crossing the street, even with the light—you'd pay attention and take precautions, especially if you saw a speeding, out-of-control car heading toward your intersection. Having a realistic idea about AIDS and its risks helps us to avoid worrying while taking appropriate care of ourselves.

Who Gets AIDS?

There is a great deal of debate about how to define the risks of AIDS today. The vast majority of PWAs are gay men, with a sizable and growing component of black and Hispanic IV drug users and their partners (mainly women). However, a small but growing percentage of PWAs are heterosexual non-IV-drug users (about 6 percent of the total). (There is also a small percentage of PWAs who were infected via blood transfusions, but thanks to improved blood screening techniques, there is only a small risk of people in the United States being infected in this way. No one can be infected with HIV by *giving* blood.)

Generally, everyone who is sexually active should take certain precautions against becoming infected with HIV. That's because even if you have only a 1 percent chance of getting it, if you do, you could still end up 100 percent dead. However, it is possible to divide behaviors into "Most Risky," "Somewhat Risky," and "Least Risky."

The Most Risky Sexual Behaviors

Here are the types of behaviors most likely to expose you to
AIDS:

- being on the receiving end of anal sex, whether you are
  a man or a woman (such behavior is extremely risky even
  with a condom);
- "fisting" (putting a fist into a rectum) or "rimming" (kissing
  a person's anus);
- having sex with a gay or bisexual man;
- sharing a needle with another IV drug user (this goes for
  cocaine injection as well as heroin use);
- having sex with someone who has been an IV drug user;
- having multiple partners (more than one partner within a
  year or so);
- having sex with someone who has multiple partners;
- sharing dildos or other sexual toys with your sexual partner;
- having vaginal sex without using a latex condom and
  spermicide;
- performing fellatio without a latex condom when the man
  comes;
- performing cunnilingus without a dental dam on a woman
  who is having her period.

All of these risks are based on the understanding that AIDS
is transmitted from one person's blood to another's, or from
one person's semen to another person's blood. Thus putting
a needle into your bloodstream when another person's
blood is already on it is a very efficient way of getting HIV
into your bloodstream if the other person's blood is infected.

Anal sex is also very risky, because the penis is likely to
rupture or tear the membranes inside the rectum. Thus the
person on the receiving end of anal sex has an "open
channel" to his or her bloodstream. If any virus is in the man's
semen, it has direct access to the "receiver's" bloodstream.
Even using condoms during anal sex is risky, since most

condoms aren't strong enough to withstand this sexual practice. If a condom breaks, semen then has clear access into any cuts or tears that lead into the bloodstream.

Likewise, putting a fist into someone's rectum is likely to tear the lining. Generally, the lining of a rectum is more sensitive than a vagina, and so is more likely to have tears and abrasions, even invisible ones. The contact between the blood in someone's rectum and possible cuts or scrapes on someone's hand or in the mouth might transmit the virus.

Having sex with a gay or bisexual man is risky simply because so many gay men have been exposed to HIV. By the same reasoning, so many IV drug users have the AIDS virus that anyone having sex with an IV drug user should take especially thorough precautions. (For more about ways to prevent HIV infection, see below.)

Having multiple partners—that is, more than one partner within a year—is risky because it exposes you to more people, thus increasing your chances of being exposed to HIV. If you have several partners within a short time, such as a month, you are also increasing the likelihood that you won't hear about it if one of the partners has symptoms of AIDS or some other STD, or if the person tests positive for HIV. By the same token, if your partner has multiple partners, you are running the same risks that he or she is running.

Sharing dildos or sex toys with a partner opens the possibility that one partner's blood or semen might end up on the object, which might then make tiny tears or cuts in the other partner's skin and pass along the virus.

Vaginal sex without a condom is risky for two reasons. The man might infect the woman by making tiny tears or abrasions inside her vagina, which then offer a channel to her bloodstream for any HIV that might be in the man's semen. Or the man might have tiny abrasions on his penis, which might then be infected by the woman's vaginal fluids. No one exactly knows to what extent a woman's vaginal fluids might pass along HIV, but as long as this is unknown, both men and women should protect themselves by using a condom. Spermicide that contains nonoxynol-9 also seems to combat the AIDS virus. Spermicide can be used in the form of foam, which a woman puts inside her vagina; cream or jelly that a woman puts inside her diaphragm; or lubricant, which a man puts inside his condom. Some condoms come with spermicidal lubricant inside them already. Other condoms have lubricants that do not contain spermicide—so read the package carefully! You're looking for the words *nonoxynol-9*, the name of the most effective spermicide. Condoms should also be made of latex. Sheepskin condoms seem to allow passage of viruses.

Performing fellatio without a condom is dangerous for both sexes if the man receiving fellatio comes. That's because, once again, the man's semen might contain HIV, which might find itself into the other person's bloodstream through tiny tears or abrasions in the person's mouth. Even brushing one's teeth might cause invisible cuts in the gums that might provide opening for HIV to infect the bloodstream through the mouth. Saliva and stomach acid seem to have some ability to "neutralize" HIV, but there are so many ways that a person's mouth might have tears or cuts that contact between semen and mouth is considered extremely risky by most experts.

Performing cunnilingus without a dental dam is dangerous if the woman is having her period, since HIV that might be in the woman's blood could enter the partner's mouth through those same tiny cuts.

Somewhat Risky Behavior

Here is another group of sexual behaviors that are not quite as risky as the ones listed above, but that still carry some risk:

- having vaginal sex with a condom and spermicide, particularly with someone you don't know well;
- performing fellatio without a condom when the man doesn't come into the partner's mouth;

- performing cunnilingus without a dental dam on a woman who isn't having her period;
- using drugs or alcohol before having sex;
- engaging in tongue kissing or "soul" kissing, especially with someone you don't know well, someone who might be an IV drug user, or someone who might be a gay or bisexual man.

Even vaginal intercourse with a condom and spermicide can carry some risk of infection with HIV. If the condom breaks, for example, or if it slips off during or after intercourse, the woman is exposed to possibly infected semen. If she knows her partner well, she may have a pretty good idea of whether he has ever used IV drugs or had sexual contact with a man. But no matter how well you think you know someone, a person might keep one or two things back from you, especially information that many men might consider embarrassing. Sometimes, too, people forget experiences that they find embarrassing, unpleasant, or likely to be misunderstood. A man might genuinely forget an early experience with IV drugs or with another man—but, remembered or not, the experience might still have exposed him to HIV.

By the same token, if a condom slips off during or after intercourse, a man's penis might come in contact with a woman's vaginal fluids or menstrual blood, exposing him to HIV in the ways we have already discussed. A woman might have had a sexual relationship with an IV drug user or a gay\bisexual man without even being aware of it. If so, no matter how honest she is with her partner or how well her partner knows her, she has still engaged in risky behavior that neither she nor her partner knows about.

Fellatio without a condom when the man doesn't come into the partner's mouth is somewhat less risky than other types of intercourse, but there is still a risk. No one is sure whether an infected person can transmit HIV through pre-orgasmic fluids (the fluids that a man's penis releases before he comes). If there is enough HIV in these fluids, they too might carry the virus into the partner's bloodstream through cuts or tears in the mouth. However, most experts consider this activity only "somewhat risky."

Cunnilingus when the woman doesn't have her period seems to be one of the safer sexual activities. The risk comes in the possibility that the woman's vaginal fluids might contain HIV. If you are performing this act with someone you know has used IV drugs, or had relationships with gay/bisexual men or IV drug users, you are taking somewhat of a risk. Likewise, if you don't know someone well, you have no way of knowing her sexual history.

Having sex after drinking or taking drugs is somewhat risky because your judgment is likely to be impaired under those circumstances. You are less likely to make sure to use a condom and spermicide, or to do so correctly; to make sure that fellatio doesn't result in the man coming into his partner's mouth; or to wait until you know someone better so you can decide how trustworthy he or she is. If your partner is drunk or high, he or she may also be less responsible, no matter how careful you are being. A man who is "under the influence" may not be as able to control when he comes, exposing his partner to semen that might contain HIV (and that might lead to pregnancy, if his partner is a woman).

Tongue kissing or "soul kissing" is generally considered a less risky activity, since the saliva in a person's mouth seems to have some ability to kill HIV. However, it's possible that the person you're kissing has sores or bleeding gums, and that the blood from the person's mouth might find its way into your bloodstream through invisible cuts or sores in your own mouth. Therefore, this is a somewhat risky activity with someone whom you don't know well or with someone who has a large chance of being infected with HIV.

Least Risky Behavior

Ideas for getting sexual pleasure without risking one's life were developed early in the AIDS crisis. Here is a list of activities that are least likely to expose you to infection with HIV:

- cuddling and hugging;
- stroking and caressing, through clothes or on bare skin;
- massage;
- kissing parts of the body other than the genitals, mouth, or anus (as long as you avoid cuts, sores, or anything that might bleed);
- sharing fantasies or talking about sexy things together;
- taking a shower or a bath together;
- masturbating yourself or each other.

There are lots of different ways you could use the activities on this list. You might use them as a way to get to know a person better, in order to decide whether you trust him or her enough to take bigger sexual risks. You might also decide, with your partner, to get tested for AIDS or other STDs, and then engage only in these activities for six months or so, until you can be tested again, putting off riskier activities until you are *sure* that neither you nor your partner is infected with HIV (or with some other STD). You might simply decide that this is the kind of sexual activity that you feel most comfortable with, for now, or you might enjoy these activities along with others on the riskier lists.

Every person must use his or her own judgment about what feels good and what feels safe in a sexual relationship. This chapter can provide you with the experts' opinions on what the risks are, but deciding how to operate with those risks is up to you. You may find that you come up with different answers at different times, depending on your age, your mood, or your partner.

Whatever you decide, though, you should be certain of one thing: STDs including AIDS, are on the rise, and no matter how much you love someone or someone loves you, it's possible to get infected or to infect someone else. Whatever you decide to do, make sure your behavior takes account of the facts.

Between Men and Women

Because the AIDS crisis in the United States was first identified in the gay male community, there has been a great deal of debate about whether HIV can be easily transmitted between men and women. Experts agree that HIV can *definitely* be transmitted in heterosexual intercourse, and it can *definitely* be transmitted both from men to women and from women to men. However, many experts disagree about the conditions under which this takes place and about how easy it is.

Most experts have suggested that it is easier for men to transmit HIV to women than for women to give it to men. That's because the penis releases semen into the woman (or into a condom within the woman's body), so by definition, the man is "passing" his bodily fluids into her. As we have seen, anal sex, even with a condom, is an extremely risky kind of sexual activity, because the walls of the rectum can tear so easily. Anal sex between men and women is just as risky as the same activity between men and men. In fact, that's a perfect example of a high-risk *behavior* that can endanger you, even if you're not in a high-risk *group*.

Vaginal sex is less risky, especially with a condom, but it still leaves the possibility that the penis might bruise or scrape the walls of the vagina. In any case, assuming that both the penis and the vagina have tiny cuts or openings, semen seems to be more likely to transmit an infection than vaginal fluids.

Men have gotten HIV from prostitutes, but some experts speculate that this is from their contact with another man's semen within the prostitutes vagina, not from her own infection with the disease.

On the other hand, a small but insistent minority believe strongly that women can easily transmit the virus to men. They agree that men are slightly more likely to pass on HIV, say, 40 percent, but they believe that the woman's chance of infecting the man is 30 percent, a relatively minor difference in their opinion.

All experts agree that the chances of infection traveling either way are greatly increased when either partner has another STD. That's because other STDs tend to leave sores or openings on the genitals, which provide easy access of HIV to the bloodstream.

Experts also agree that having multiple partners increases both sexes' chance of getting infected. That's because the more encounters you have, the more chance you have of being involved with someone who is infected. In one study, gay men who had AIDS reported 1,100 partners over their lifetimes, as opposed to 500 partners for gay men without AIDS and 25 partners for heterosexuals.

On the other hand, remember our example of running onto a crowded freeway at night in the rain—the more you do it, the greater your chances of getting hit by a car. Nevertheless, doing it even one time is by definition a risky activity—and if you were careless or unlucky enough to get hit the first time instead of the 20th, you'd still be just as dead.

How Can You Prevent AIDS?

Here is a list of suggestions for how to avoid being infected with the HIV. If there is any way that a suggestion can be made to apply to you, you should consider following it. As we've said countless times before, AIDS is not just a problem for "high-risk groups." It's a concern for anyone—gay or straight—who engages in high-risk *behaviors*.

- For vaginal sex, use latex condoms (natural sheepskin ones might allow the virus to work its way through) and spermicide that contains nonoxynol-9 (the woman might

use foam with this ingredient, or she might use a diaphragm with jelly or cream that contains it, or the man
might buy a condom lubricated with spermicide that
includes this ingredient, or he might buy lubricant that
includes it and put it inside the condom).

- Avoid anal sex, fisting, rimming, or an activity that puts you
  in contact with your partner's semen, blood, feces, or urine.
- Don't share dildos or any other object that gets inserted into
  a person's body.
- Avoid multiple or anonymous partners. Take extreme precautions with people who have had multiple or anonymous
  partners and people who have had PWAs or people who are
  HIV positive as partners.
- Don't have any kind of sex—oral, anal, or vaginal—with an
  infected partner, an IV drug user, or a person who has had
  sex with either of those two.
- Avoid open-mouth kissing with an infected partner, an IV
  drug user, or a person who has had sex with either of those
  two.
- Don't use Vaseline or petroleum jelly as a lubricant; it
  might irritate the penis or vagina and create openings
  through which you could be infected; it might also destroy
  the latex on a condom. Use water-based lubricants only.
- Don't share needles with anyone.
- Don't use "poppers"—inhaled amyl or isobutyl—and
  don't use heroin; they seem to contribute to the suppres-
  sion of the immune system (as well as affecting your
  judgment).
- Don't douche just before or just after sex; it suppresses the
  body's own cleansing mechanism.
- A diaphragm with spermicide that contains nonoxynol-9
  can help catch a woman's menstrual blood and keep it
  away from her partner (although this is not a completely
  foolproof method).
- Be aware that your partner might not be telling you the
  full truth, either deliberately or because he or she doesn't
  remember an incident that might affect your safety.

- Remember that you are a valuable person who has the right both to sexual pleasure and to staying alive!

AIDS and Gay Sex

Because AIDS in the United States was first diagnosed in the gay community, it gave rise to a lot of myths and rumors. Because many people already disapproved of gay sex as "sinful" or "unnatural," they tended to see this terrible disease as "God's punishment" or as the "natural" outcome of certain sexual practices. Some spoke of AIDS as a heaven-sent plague. Some people who were prejudiced against gay people used their fear of AIDS as an excuse to increase the violent attacks on gay people, with or without AIDS.

In fact, AIDS in Africa and Haiti is primarily a heterosexual disease. How and why AIDS spreads has to do with the specific ways the virus works, not with anything "sinful" or "unnatural" about a particular kind of sex.

As we have seen, AIDS is easily transmitted by anal sex, a type of sex practiced by both gay and straight men. AIDS is also more easily transmitted among people who have other STDs, people who use "poppers" or other drugs that suppress the immune system, and people who have multiple partners. These factors were true of many people in the gay community in the United States in the 1970s, but they were not true of all gay men, then or now. There is nothing "natural" or obvious about the relationship between gay sex and AIDS; it just happens to be the way things worked out. In fact, when gay men realized the health risks they were running, many were able to modify their behavior while continuing to have enjoyable and satisfying relationships.

AIDS is a frightening disease. Some people may feel less frightened by making up stories about it to explain why some people "deserve" it. Of course, even those stories don't explain why the children of mothers infected with AIDS should be born sick, or why a person who gets a blood transfusion should develop the disease. But dividing up people who "deserve" a disease and people who don't "deserve" it is as ridiculous as trying to figure out the "innocent" and "guilty" victims of an earthquake or a flood. AIDS is a tragic disease caused by a virus. This disease will become even more tragic if some people are allowed to use it as an excuse for prejudice, discrimination, or violence against others.

Keeping a Perspective on AIDS

The gay male community among whom AIDS was first discovered in the U.S. has significantly moderated its behavior to have safer forms of sex. Sadly, however, the younger generation of gay men, straight people, and IV drug users are not all taking the epidemic seriously. Somehow, many young people believe that the AIDS crisis just doesn't apply to them.

Believe it or not, it does. The Centers for Disease Control released a report noting that AIDS among 13- to 19-year-olds increased by 61 percent between February 1988 and 1989. Since the epidemic began, more than 5,000 children and young adults have died of AIDS, according to the August 3, 1992 *Newsweek*, which also points out that AIDS is now the sixth leading cause of death among 15- to 24-year-olds.

Colonel Donald Burke of Walter Reed Army Medical Center also notes an increase of danger to teenagers. He points out that one out of every 3,000 teenage applicants for U.S. military service now tests positive for HIV. If children are infected with HIV, they may well have AIDS within six to 11 years by the time they are teenagers. According to Colonel Burke, "[Our information] suggests that HIV is a real and immediate threat to teenagers throughout the United States."

Newsweek points out that between 1989 and 1992, the cumulative number of 13- to 24-year-olds diagnosed with AIDS increased 77 percent (that is, the number went up as new cases were added to the total). Nearly half of the teenagers with AIDS come from just six places—New York, New Jersey, Texas, California, Florida, and Puerto Rico—so teens in those areas should be especially aware that their friends or classmates might be infected, maybe without even knowing it. The other half of AIDS cases is spread throughout almost every state plus the District of Columbia. Living in a rural area or a small town is no protection.

What is frightening about the statistics is that they show such a rapid increase in such a few years. The same August 1992 *Newsweek* cites the work of Dr. Lawrence D'Angelo, a Washington, D.C. doctor who tested blood samples from the Children's National Medical Center, a large city public hospital. Looking at the samples of 13- to 20-year-olds between October 1987 and January 1989, only one in 250 tested HIV positive. From January 1989 through October 1991, the rate was up to one in 90. D'Angelo predicts that the next batch of figures will show the rate as one in 50.

Tests of college students reveal similar increases. A 1990 study of blood samples from college students on 19 campuses showed one student in 500 was HIV positive. In 1991, another test was taken among 137,000 Job Corps participants—and the rate was almost one in 300. Even though these figures really aren't comparable, because they were drawn from two different places, they do reveal that even middle-class, educated kids are getting infected with HIV, not simply the stereotypical "inner-city drug user."

As the figures rise, more women are becoming infected, probably from their heterosexual male partners. U.S. Surgeon General Antonia Novello says that in 1987, women made up only 17 percent of adolescent cases—rising to 39 percent in 1991.

Ironically, the figures for transmission of AIDS by heterosexual contact are much higher for young people than they are for people in their late 20s and early 30s. Heterosexual contact has generated only 6 percent of all AIDS cases—but 12 percent of all AIDS cases among 13- to 24-year-olds. Overall, AIDS strikes nine times as many men as women— but for 13- to 24-year-olds, the ratio is only four to one. This suggests both that teenagers are a lot less careful than older people, and that, as a result, teenagers are more likely to find their friends and classmates to be infected with HIV.

The sad possibility of "slipping just once" was noted by Pat Christen, director of the San Francisco AIDS Foundation. She quoted one AIDS patient's story: "I practiced only safe sex since 1987. I was not infected and made a strong commitment to myself to stay uninfected. Unfortunately, several months ago I slipped once and engaged in high-risk sex. I have never done it since, but I just found out I am now infected. After so many years, I slipped once. I hope you can get to others so it's not too late for them."

Amy Dolph, quoted in the August 3, 1992 *Newsweek*, had a similar experience. She grew up in the small town of Katy, Texas, in a family that could afford to send her to college. She was the last of her friends to lose her virginity, and, she says, she didn't sleep around. But the second man she slept with gave her HIV, and now she, too, is at risk of dying from AIDS. Dolph says she knew that the man who infected her had experimented with drugs, but she didn't find out he was bisexual until later.

When Dolph found out in 1987 that she was HIV positive, she was only a senior in high school. "Every one of my dreams was shattered, blown away," Dolph says. She wishes she had known more: "Back then we were always reading that you're only at high risk if you're this group, this group or this group. And you're at low risk if you're a sexually active heterosexual. And everyone saw that 'low risk' as 'no risk.'"

Dolph wants to warn other teenagers not to make her mistake. She says, "Do you want to put your life in that other person's hands? Is that boy or girl worth dying for? I doubt it."

Finally, here's a message from author Randy Shilts, who chronicled the history of AIDS in his book, *And the Band Played On*. Shilts, a gay activist, was quoted in the February 23, 1988 *Village Voice* as saying, "The situation does not require panic, but it does require prudence. Any heterosexual woman who doesn't demand that her sex partner use a condom is being a bimbo, because you may be that one in 10,000 AIDS cases coming from a singles bar, and if you become that person, you will be 100 per cent dead. . . . The great mistake gay men made was not taking this disease seriously until someone they knew died, and by then it was too late. With heterosexuals, sometimes I want to shake them and say, my God, don't make the same mistake."

5

What You Don't Know Can Hurt You

Elise and Martin are usually pretty happy with their new relationship, but sometimes each one is dissatisfied or worried, still. Every month, Elise gets nervous as she waits for her period, even though she and Martin use condoms and foam. Still, sometimes—not very often, but sometimes—they don't get the condom on in time, or Elise forgets to bring the foam with her. She worries about getting pregnant. She also worries that if Martin has been with anybody else, she could be exposing herself to a big risk. After all, if the two of them don't even use protection properly all the time, how does she know he's being careful with other people?

Even though he'd never admit it, Martin also worries about Elise getting pregnant. He sure isn't ready to be a father! He knows that Elise was a virgin when he first slept with her, but he has been with a couple of other girls since then—just once—but he's pretty sure they were much more experienced than Elise. He didn't feel as comfortable with them as he did with Elise, so he didn't have the same conversation ahead of time—they just did it. Every so often, he thinks about the risk he took.

Charlie and Richard are finding ways to talk about what they want to do together and how they want to handle their relationship. Even though they both tested negative, they have decided to be very careful with each other and with other people, so that neither one of them gets sick in the future. Charlie says he really doesn't mind if Richard goes on seeing other guys once in a while, as long as Richard promises that he's taking precautions, and as long as he and Charlie take precautions, too. So they've agreed: They'll always use condoms and spermicide, they'll avoid anal sex, and every six months, they'll both get tested, to keep making sure they're healthy. Both of them know that it won't be easy to stick to this agreement—especially Richard!—but both of them realize that it's important to do it anyway. "I love you," says Richard, "and I don't want to be the reason that anything bad happens to you."

Marisol and Robert decide that they really can't agree on the terms of their relationship. Sadly, they break up. Robert decides that he doesn't really want another relationship right now. He thinks he'll be happier just seeing girls occasionally, without letting anything get serious. Now he knows, though, that that's a lot riskier than being in a steady, monogamous relationship, so he's going to be sure to use condoms and foam, to find out about his partner's health and history, and to avoid anal sex.

Marisol is very sad without Robert for a few months. Then she finds another man she likes who also wants an exclusive relationship. The two of them don't talk about their sexual histories right away. But after they've had a couple of sessions of kissing and making out, they realize they'd both like to go further. Marisol talks about Robert, Robert's history of having several partners, and the PID she had. The other man shares his history, too. Then together, they decide what activities they feel comfortable with and what precautions they're going to take.

Taking Care of Yourself

Throughout this book, we've talked about various risks and dangers that you may be exposed to from different sexually transmitted diseases. In this chapter, we'll summarize some of the best ways to protect yourself from STDs, along with information about birth control. Since many of your best protections involve talking with your partner, we've included a section with some suggestions for ways to do that. Because all of your protections are based on your making decisions that you yourself are comfortable with, we've included some suggestions for thinking about your decisions, too. Finally, STDs are everybody's problem, thus we've ended with some ideas for taking action, on your own, in your school, and in your community.

Taking Precautions

How can you prevent being infected with STDs? Here are some suggestions:

- The only really safe sex is no sex. That's a sad fact of life, but it's true. If you're sure you're ready for a sexual relationship, going without sex completely may not be a good option for you. But if you think that you're not ready yet, the risks you're taking are just one more reason to stick to your guns, follow your heart, and do only what's right for you.

- The following activities are the safest kinds of sexual contact: closed-mouth kissing; massage, touching, and caressing, with or without clothes, but avoiding genitals, mouth, anus, and any sores or bleeding places; sharing fantasies; taking a shower or a bath together.
- The following activities are somewhat more risky kinds of sexual contact, but if you know that your partner is not HIV positive, a drug user, or someone with a long history of many anonymous partners, you may be willing to take the risk: open-mouth kissing; masturbating next to or against your partner (as long as the man makes sure his semen is nowhere near the woman's genitals); masturbating your partner through clothes; fellatio as long as the man doesn't come in his partner's mouth; cunnilingus as long as the woman isn't having her period.
- Vaginal sex with a condom and spermicide is risky, too, but being very sure always to use a condom and spermicide with nonoxynol-9 (either as foam, as diaphragm cream or jelly, or as lubricant) reduces the risks somewhat. Be sure, too, that you and your partner know the right way to use a condom (see below for more information).
- The following activities are so risky that most experts believe that they should be avoided completely: anal sex under any circumstances, fisting, rimming, any kind of activity that causes a partner to bleed, vaginal sex without a condom and spermicide, sharing dildos or other sex toys, any other kind of activity that involves contact between one person's bloodstream and the other person's blood or semen.
- Know the symptoms of the various STDs and check yourself and your partner for signs of them. Never do *anything* with someone who has open sores or pimples in the mouth or genital area, and never do anything with someone while you yourself have these symptoms. If something about your partner concerns you, ask. It might make you feel embarrassed, but which would you rather be, embarrassed or dead? Embarrassed or never able to

have children? Embarrassed or always having to tell *your* partners that you might infect *them*?

- Respect yourself and your partner enough to take care of yourself and be honest. You deserve good relationships that give you pleasure, and so does your partner. Don't do anything you don't feel comfortable with, and don't pressure anyone else.
- If you think you've been exposed to HIV, get tested. You might think "you'd rather not know," but there are two very good reasons for knowing: (1) you might be able to get treatment and to take better care of yourself, which could make a big difference in your life and health. Even though there's no cure for AIDS yet, there maybe ways to keep HIV from turning into AIDS. (2) Your partners have a right to know whether you're infected or not. You can still have some types of sexual contact after you've got HIV, but you should take extra precautions, for your own sake as well as your partner's.

Using a Condom

Using a condom can seem scary if you've never done it, but once you know how, it's easy and it can even be fun! Both men and women have said that putting a condom on a man can be enjoyable, part of the play in getting ready to actually have sex. Since you really have no choice if you care about your health, you might as well make the condom a part of the fun rather than a chore to avoided.

A condom can only be put on an erect penis. However, a penis can certainly get harder after a condom is already on it, so you don't have to wait until the last minute to put it on. Most couples find that it helps to have condoms nearby, so that when the time is right, they are at hand.

If you've bought condoms that are already lubricated with spermicide containing nonoxynol-9, that may also make things simpler. However, if a woman has sex with a man, she should use foam or a diaphragm along with the condom, whether it is lubricated with spermicide or not. A condom alone is just not enough protection for a woman. A woman can put foam or a diaphragm into her vagina up to two hours before intercourse starts.

When you take a condom out of the package, you'll see that it is flat, with a little rubber ring. As you slide that rubber ring down over the penis, rolling it gently and carefully so as not to tear the condom, the penis is gradually covered in a little latex sheath, like a long, thin plastic bag. Be sure to pinch the tip of the condom as you put it on, so that about a half-inch or so remains at the tip of the penis. Then, when the man comes, that part of the condom will fill up. If you don't leave that extra room, the man's coming could force the condom off or even break it.

After the man has come, he should withdraw his penis from his partner, gently and carefully, before he gets completely soft. Otherwise, the condom might come off inside the other person, leaving the man's semen inside. (If this does happen, of course, you can easily get the condom out—but you have had no protection against STDs or pregnancy. That's why also using spermicide is so important.) As the man withdraws his penis, he should keep hold of the condom's rim, to make sure it stays on his penis. The full condom can be thrown in the garbage or flushed down the toilet. The man should wash his hands to make sure he has no semen on them before touching the other person.

If you're a guy, you can practice using a condom once or twice when you masturbate, so that you feel completely comfortable with the procedure. If you're a woman, you can practice putting a condom on a carrot or banana. It might seem silly—but you'll be less nervous with practice!

Birth Control

Condoms and foam will do more than prevent STDs. They'll also help prevent pregnancy. However, there are some even more effective birth control methods, which woman might also want to consider. (Condoms are only 75 percent to 90 percent effective in preventing pregnancy. The effectiveness range is so wide because people who use condoms may not use them every time or may not always use them correctly.)

Diaphragm

The diaphragm is a rubber cup that is filled with cream or jelly containing spermicide. It fits inside the woman's vagina, over her cervix (when you put it in right, you can feel the little bone of the cervix behind the rubber cup), and prevents semen from getting into the uterus and exposing any semen that does get in to spermicide. The diaphragm also catches the woman's blood during her period. Although it is not a completely safe way to prevent partners from exposure to menstrual blood (men should still use condoms during vaginal intercourse; men and women should still use dental dams during cunnilingus), it is an added precaution.

A diaphragm can be put in up to two hours before intercourse starts and must stay in for at least six hours after intercourse is over. It can sometimes be shaken out of place by certain sexual positions, such as if the woman is on top or if the couple is standing up. It might also shift if the woman moves her bowels, in which case a woman should check to make sure her diaphragm is still in place.

As we have seen, the diaphragm can be some protection against STDs other than AIDS, because it helps prevent semen from entering the uterus. Many women these days like to use both diaphragm plus spermicide *and* condoms. That way, they are getting the maximum protection against both STDs and pregnancy.

A diaphragm can be bought at a drugstore, but it must be fitted by a doctor or health worker at a clinic. Some of the agencies listed in Chapter 7 will help teenaged girls obtain diaphragms.

Cervical Caps

The cervical cap is a small rubber device that fits over the woman's cervix, preventing pregnancy by blocking sperm from entering the uterus. Like the diaphragm, the cap must be fitted by a doctor; also like the diaphragm, the woman can put the device in and take it out by herself. Again like the diaphragm, the cervical cap must be used with spermicidal cream or jelly, but unlike the diaphragm, spermicide doesn't need to be reinserted for each sexual act, since the cap fits so snugly that it holds the spermicide in place.

According to the National Institutes of Health, the cervical cap is 85 percent effective in preventing pregnancy—comparable to the diaphragm. Some of the 15 percent failure rate is attributable to incorrect use of the device or failure to use it all the time. That means that if you use a cervical cap every time you have intercourse and use it correctly ever time, its effectiveness rate is actually very high, more than 95 percent. (This is also comparable to the diaphragm.)

The cap can remain in the woman's body for 48 hours. Like the diaphragm, it seems to provide partial protection against the AIDS virus and other STDs if it's used with spermicide containing nonoxynol-9. Nevertheless, as with the diaphragm, experts recommend using condoms to protect against disease, even if they are not needed for birth control.

Birth Control Pills

"The pill" is one of the most foolproof methods of birth control, although even it occasionally fails. There are various types of birth control pills. All affect a woman's hormones, preventing her from getting pregnant by altering her body chemistry. Some women may experience some negative side effects, such as mood changes, weight gain, headaches, nausea, or more difficulty with their periods, more intense cramps, or bleeding in between their periods. On the other hand, some women report positive side effects such as easier and less painful periods.

The pill should definitely not be taken by any woman with a family history of migraine headaches, high blood pressure, or circulatory problems. For those women, the pill might actually be dangerous, leading to heart attack, stroke, or other problems. The pill is also not recommended for women who smoke or are over the age of 35.

Birth-control pills come in different strengths and different combinations of hormones and must be prescribed by a doctor. If your doctor has prescribed birth-control pills for you, you may need to work with him or her to make sure that you are getting the type of pill that best suits you. Sometimes doctors don't take women's and girls' complaints seriously in this regard, so be sure to stand up for yourself. You have a right to birth control without unpleasant or dangerous side effects.

Most birth control pills are taken either every day or every day in a month but seven (the seven days of your period). If you forget to take a pill one day, you might be taking the risk of getting pregnant. However, birth-control pills are one of the most effective methods of preventing pregnancy, most types of pills have a 97 percent to 99 percent effectiveness rate.

If you feel most comfortable taking the pill to prevent pregnancy, remember that it provides no protection at all against STDs. You may still need to use condoms and foam in addition to taking the pill.

Norplant and Depo-Provera

Other hormonal methods of birth control that are very effective are *Norplant* and *Depo-Provera*. Effectiveness rates for these methods are 99 percent. Norplant is a series of toothpick-sized rods that are placed underneath the skin and release small amounts of hormones. Since these implants last for five years, they are recommended for those who might forget to take birth-control pills on a regular schedule.

Depo-Provera is a single shot of hormones that can prevent pregnancy over a period of three months.

While Norplant and Depo-Provera provide effective birth control, condoms are still needed for protection against STDs during sex.

Other Types of Birth Control

There are other types of birth control, but these tend to be either dangerous or less effective. The IUD, or intrauterine device, fits inside the woman's uterus. It must be fitted by a doctor, and it must be taken out by a doctor. Its advantage is that it stays inside the woman permanently (for several years), unlike the diaphragm, which has to be inserted, and, unlike the pill, it doesn't affect a woman's body chemistry and is safe for women with migraine or high blood pressure. However, it too may have side effects, including cramping and heavier periods. Some women have also been injured by their IUDs, and IUDs are believed to increase the risk of PID. Generally, they are not recommended for teenagers, especially not for women who have never had a child.

Like the diaphragm, the sponge fits inside a woman's vagina, up against her cervix. It is full of spermicide that is activated by moistening the sponge before insertion. Teenaged girls may find it easier to insert the sponge than the diaphragm, both physically and emotionally, since the sponge can go in up to 24 hours before intercourse.

However, the sponge is simply not as effective in preventing pregnancy as the diaphragm. Also, many women report vaginal infections and irritations from contraceptive sponges.

Talking with Your Partner

Throughout this book, we've stressed the importance of talking with your partner about what you're doing, what you want, and what you feel comfortable with. We've also talked about knowing your partner. That doesn't mean knowing whether he likes horror movies or whether she gets along well with her brothers and sisters (although these can be important in a relationship for other reasons!). It means knowing your partner's sexual history, so that you have a realistic idea of what risks you might be exposed to.

Here are some things that it's important to know about your partner:

1. How many people he or she has had sex with;
2. Whether a man has had any sexual experiences with men;
3. Whether he or she has ever used IV drugs or had sexual contact (even just kissing) with someone who has used IV drugs;
4. What kind of precautions the person has taken in earlier sexual relationships; was a condom and spermicide always used in sex involving men? Was a dental dam always used in oral sex with women? Does the person understand the dangers of contact with blood and semen? What kinds of experiences has he or she had that involved that kind of contact?

Of course, when you ask your partner these questions, you have only his or her word that the truth is being told. You have to use your own judgment, too—which is why it's so important to take precautions with your partner, even if you get the "right" answer to every question. After all, your partner might have different ideas than you about what's "safe" or even what's true! He or she might think it's all right to lie "in a good cause" or "out of love for you." He or she might also genuinely not remember certain experiences, or might genuinely not know or be mistaken about certain information (like whether a previous partner used IV drugs or was bisexual).

It's also important to talk with your partner about the terms of your relationship. Are you going to be sexual only with each other, or will one or both of you have other partners? Will these other partners be steady relationships or one-night stands? Will each of you commit to having sex only with precautions, or is one of you likely to have unprotected sex with someone else? Knowing the answers to these questions will help you decide what risks you're taking by being sexual with this person, so that you can decide what precautions you want to take with him or her.

It might seem uncomfortable to talk about these questions, but remember, you just don't know what's going to happen after you start having a sexual relationship. You might assume that if the person loves you as much as he or she says, you'll be the only partner. Your partner might have quite different assumptions—even if he or she is totally sincere about loving you. Or your partner might promise one thing and then do another, with or without intending to. Even if your partner later apologizes for a terrible mistake, what good will the apology do if you have already been exposed to a sexually transmitted disease? Isn't it better, especially in the early stages of a relationship, to protect yourself as well as trusting your partner?

Even if you don't discuss your past relationships and history with your partner, you can still have some measure of protection by making sure to use a condom. As we have seen, using a condom isn't as effective a means of protection as not having sex in the first place—but it is the next best thing.

If you're a man who wants to use a condom, you can make sure that you have some condoms with you if you think you might be having sex. If you have one ready to use, you may not even have to talk about it, if you find that uncomfortable.

What if you want your partner to use a condom? If you've been able to talk about your sexual histories and the rules of your relationship, you can always discuss future precautions at that time. Even if you haven't had that larger conversation, however, you can still insist that any man you're intimate with wear a condom for vaginal, anal, or oral sex—especially if you've brought your own condoms with you.

Here are some ways you might want to open the discussion *before* things get intimate:

"These days, I think it's safest if you use a condom—that way, neither of us has to worry."

"I don't want to have to worry about either of us—so I'd like you to wear a condom."

"I think condoms are sexy—I hope you're planning to wear one."

You may find it more awkward to open the discussion *after* things have gotten intimate—but it's still not too late— here are some possibilities:

"Would you please use this?"

"I have something for you."

"I don't want to worry—here."

Unfortunately, a lot of guys still think it's less "manly" to wear condoms. They may also be concerned with how a condom interferes with their sexual pleasure. Some people—guys or girls—are insulted by the idea that the guy should wear a condom; they see it as suggesting that they are not "clean." If your partner brings up one of these objections, stick to your guns. You might find it easier to keep repeating a short phrase, rather than getting drawn into a long argument; for example, you might just say, "I'll worry too much to enjoy myself if you don't wear one," or "These days, no one is safe without wearing a condom," or even "This is the only way I'm willing to go ahead."

Finally, you may also want to talk to your partner about what does and doesn't feel good sexually. This sharing is an important part of a sexual relationship, whether or not you're actually having intercourse. If, for example, you're happy with kissing, but your partner wants to go further, you might need to say "No" or "Stop." Whether or not you want to have intercourse or oral sex with your partner, you might want him or her to touch you in different ways or in different places, so that you will enjoy the experience more.

Here are some ways for talking about sex with your partner that might be helpful or give you some ideas for finding your own words:

- "I really like you, but I don't want to go that far."
- "Stop that right now—I don't like it!"
- "I liked what we did before, but I don't think I'm ready to do it again. Let's just go more slowly."
- "I really like you a lot, but I'm not ready to do that with you yet."
- "That feels great."
- "You know what I really like? When you touch me, here, really gently."
- "I really like doing this with you, but I don't like this one part of it. I'd like it better if you. . ."
- "You know what would feel really good? If you would. . ."

Sometimes it helps to express your feelings in actions as well as words. If you don't like something, you might want to gently push your partner's hand away. Even better, if you can gently guide your partner's hand or mouth to the places that you do like, showing him or her what gives you pleasure. Many people get a little nervous letting their partners know what they do and don't like, but if you can get past the nervousness, both of you can enjoy yourself and each other a lot more.

There is a stereotype in our society that guys are supposed to want sex all the time while women never do. Because of this stereotype, and because women are the ones who can get pregnant, it has often been up to the woman to say "No." If you're a woman, that might make it hard for you to enjoy sexual sharing, to admit that you enjoy it, or to stand up for yourself about what you do and don't like. If you're a guy, that might make it hard for you to take a woman seriously when she lets you know what she does and doesn't want. Both men and women should re-member that all human beings have the capacity to enjoy sex—and the right to do the things that give them pleasure.

On the other hand, there is also a stereotype that says that "guys are always ready" or that if a guy is a good lover, he will automatically know what a woman likes. But, like women, each guy has his own internal clock that tells him when he is ready for what. And, like all people, guys can't read their partners' minds. They may need to be helped to understand what a particular partner wants or needs.

Finally, because of the amount of prejudice and dis-crimination faced by gay people in our society, homosex-ual men and women may feel nervous or embarrassed talking about their sexual feelings, even with a sexual partner. If you find you have difficulty talking to your partner about sex, you might start a conversation by putting *that* feeling into words: "I feel funny talking about our relationship, but I'd like to. How about you?" Talking about what the two of you are doing and what you've already done is important both to your pleasure and to your safety. If you can share your feelings of discomfort with your partner, it might even bring the two of you closer!

Making the Decisions that Are Right for You

Making decisions that you'll feel good about living with is part of learning to be an adult. If you're old enough to have sexual feelings, you're old enough to start deciding how to live with them.

Only you can tell what decisions you'll feel good about—and these decisions may change from day to day, or as circumstances change in your life. You may find yourself changing your mind, becoming more ready to have a more sexual relationship, or deciding that you've gone further than you want to go, for now.

To help you in this ongoing process of decision-making, here are some pros and cons about sexual relationships. They apply to all kinds of sexual relationships, from kissing to intercourse. A romantic kiss with someone who used to be a good friend can really change the relationship, even if that's as far as you go. Having intercourse with someone, even if you've already done everything else but, can also change the relationship. That's why it's so important for you to think about the likely consequences and choose the ones you want. And, if you find that you've been hit by consequences that you didn't want, you must decide what to do about that, too.

Good Things that Can Happen from Being Sexual with Someone:
- Feeling pleasure
- Feeling closer to the person
- Feeling good about yourself and your body
- Learning more about yourself and the other person
- Getting a more serious, more involved, and more valuable relationship.

Bad Things that Can Happen from Being Sexual with Someone:
- Not enjoying the experience
- Feeling more distant from the person
- Feeling bad about yourself and your body
- Losing a good friend because you each want different things or because you broke up

- Finding out that the person just wanted to use you for sex, or spread stories about what the two of you did
- Getting the woman pregnant—or one or both of you worrying each month that she's pregnant
- Getting a sexually transmitted disease

Even people who have been having sexual relationships for years find themselves making mistakes and changing their minds about what they do and don't want to do sexually. You'll probably make your share of mistakes along with the rest of us. Just be sure that you're not letting yourself in for mistakes that don't give you a second chance to try again later.

Taking Action

We've talked about taking personal responsibility for your own decisions. But STDs aren't just your problem—they're a problem that all of us in this society share. Sometimes the best way to face a problem is to take action. Here are some suggestions of ways that you might take action to deal with this problem, by yourself, at school, or in your community. Can you think of others?

By Yourself:
- Find out where counseling and health care are available; talk to a counselor or a doctor whom you trust.
- Read a book or a pamphlet with the information that you need.
- Share your information with a friend who needs it; find a friend who gives you good advice and support.
- Call a hot line and talk about your concerns.

At School:
- With other students, make sure your health classes include useful, up-to-date information. If you think kids won't listen

to the things teachers are saying, figure out why and propose suggestions to your school administration, maybe in the form of a petition signed by lots of students, or as an editorial in the school paper.

- Make sure other students know where health-care and information can be found. Ideally, your school counselors make this information available, but if they don't, what are the alternatives?
- Work with parents' groups, if possible, to make sure your school is doing everything possible to get students the help and information that they need.

In Your Community:

- Write a letter to the editor of a local paper about STDs and what you think should be done about them.
- Work with community groups to get good health care and counseling in your community. What do you think should be done about STDs spread through prostitution and IV drug use? What kind of laws and programs do you support? Find out what you think and then work with others to get your opinions accepted.

STDs are an enormous problem, and right now, the problem is only getting bigger. It's up to all of us to do what we can to protect ourselves, our partners, and our communities. Thinking about this problem can feel difficult, frightening, and upsetting. But not thinking about it can cost you your pleasure, your safety, and your life. Do whatever you have to do to take good care of yourself. After all, you're worth it!

6

Getting Help

Every month, Elise finds herself getting concerned about becoming pregnant. She decides to go to a clinic to discuss birth-control options as well as to make sure she's doing everything she can to protect herself against STDs. But when she thinks about actually going to talk to someone, she gets nervous, and all sorts of questions come up. How will she find a clinic? How does she make an appointment? Will she need to pay? Will they tell her parents? Elise isn't even sure how to answer these questions, much less how to get help.

Charlie and Richard decide that they should go to someone for counseling about protecting their health. They want to find a counselor who will accept their relationship, and whom they can trust to give them the latest unbiased information. They think it would be good to see a counselor as a couple, so that both of them can share responsibility for staying safe and healthy. At the same time, Richard hates the idea of exposing their relationship to a stranger, and Charlie isn't sure that a counselor can really be trusted not to try to change their behavior.

Marisol's new partner starts noticing a few symptoms that make him nervous. Even though he and Marisol have been careful, he knows that she once had PID, and he's afraid that somehow she might have infected him. He doesn't even want to tell Marisol about his suspicions—but he's not sure how to get information, or how to get treatment if he is infected. He's worried that a doctor might make him tell about his former girlfriends—or even tell his parents.

Taking Responsibility

Taking responsibility for getting the help or information you need can be scary sometimes. Once you make up your mind to take this step, however, you may feel relieved. Figuring out the type of help you need and finding ways to get it are part of the process of growing up. When you were little, you probably depended on your parents and family members for all the help you needed. You may still be able to do that—or you may need to turn elsewhere as well. Being grown up doesn't mean doing without help—it means getting yourself the help you need.

The first thing to remember when thinking about getting help or information about STDs is to never give up. If you can go to a parent, a family member, a friend of the family, a religious leader, or another trusted adult, start there. If you feel that you can't turn to those people, or if they will not or cannot give you the help you need, keep trying. Don't stop looking until you find the clinic, the counselor, the doctor, or the agency that offers what you're looking for.

Of course, you may not hear the answers you'd *like* to get. You may find out that, in fact, your sexual practices have been unsafe and that to protect yourself, you're going to have to change your behavior to some extent. You might discover that you have an STD that will require treatment, or one that you will have to tell future partners about, or one that has permanent consequences, such as difficulty having children. These may be hard facts that you'll just have to accept.

It may also be a reality that in your community, it's particularly difficult to find affordable, confidential treatment. If this unfortunate situation is the case, you may have to make some hard choices, about paying for appropriate help, traveling further than is convenient, putting more effort into finding good help, or accepting help that is not really appropriate to your needs. In general, however, this is the kind of help that you should be able to expect:

- **Affordable**—Many communities have some form of free or low-cost treatment for STDs, as well as clinics that offer birth control, give information about prevention of STDs, and provide other kinds of help and counseling on sexual issues.
- **Confidential**—Rules differ from clinic to clinic, community to community. In many places, however, the person whom you're talking to will not tell your parents or any other authority. If you have an STD, they may be legally required to ask you about other sexual partners and to notify them of your condition, so that they can get tested and, if necessary, treatment. However, in many places, even this aspect of treatment is voluntary. If you are particularly worried about confidentiality, it may also be possible to visit a clinic under an assumed name. In any case, a reputable clinic, agency, doctor, or counselor will tell you exactly what you can expect in the way of confidentiality if you ask—so if this is a concern, find out what the policy is when you are making the appointment or dropping in for your first visit.
- **Respectful**—Doctors, counselors, and other health professionals should treat you as a person who deserves respect. Even if they are bound to point out to you what they see as dangers in your behavior—such as having sex

without a condom, or engaging in high-risk sexual practices like anal sex—they should do so in a nonjudgmental
way. In this far from perfect world, you may decide that
it's worth it to you to accept help from someone whom
you feel is disrespectful or judgmental, but ideally, you
should be able to get help from someone who is able both
to tell you some hard truths and to treat you with caring
and respect.

Deciding What You Need

Many different types of help are available to someone who
is concerned about STDs. Not all of these may be available
in your community, or they may exist there but be hard to
find. In most big cities, however, you should be able to find
all of them, and even smaller cities and rural areas are
increasingly served by the following:

Doctors

You may trust your family doctor to give you help, advice,
or treatment for an STD. Or you may be able to locate
another private doctor in your community. Most doctors are
familiar with the basic health and prevention issues concern-
ing STDs; they may not be as comfortable with or as skilled
at counseling young people on making sexual choices. Most
doctors do charge a fee for their services, although you may
be able to find doctors who offer free or reduced-cost
services under some circumstances.

Clinics

A clinic is an organization that includes many doctors,
nurses, physicians' assistants, and other health-care professionals. Generally, clinics are set up to offer free or low-cost
medical care to people who can't afford private doctors. A
clinic may have certain requirements; you may need to show
proof of residence in a certain community, for example, or

show evidence that your income is below a certain level. Some clinics will not accept young people without a parental consent form. However, many clinics will accept young people for little or no money, no questions asked. There are also many clinics that specialize in offering information and treatment for STDs and other sexual issues.

Counselors

A counselor is someone who specializes in helping people talk about their concerns and make important decisions. A counselor may be a licensed therapist or simply someone who has experience with a particular issue. Counseling may be for individuals, for couples, or for groups of people that share a similar problem (such as young people concerned about sexual issues). Counseling may be one-time, short-term (once a week for less than six months), or long-term (once or twice a week for more than six months).

Generally, clinics that offer treatment for STDs also offer counseling. Their services may range from a one-time half-hour conversation about basic sexual information to a series of meetings in which a young person can get help making up his or her mind about a difficult decision. You might also approach a public or private social-service agency, which frequently offer free or low-cost counseling services.

Finding the Help You Need

Once you've decided what you want, how do you get it? Here are some suggestions:

• Check the phone book. Look first in the part of the directory that deals with city, state, and county services (usually the blue pages). There may be a hot line or information listing for STDs, AIDS, or birth control. Even if the hot line doesn't seem to be exactly what you're looking for, the people on the other end are usually able to make *referrals*—other places to look.

- Call one of the agencies listed in the final chapter of this book. Even if they are in another community, they may be able to help you find something in your own region.
- Ask your school counselor, your family doctor, a religious leader, or a sympathetic adult.

Talking to Your "Helper"

Once you've located a source of help, what should you do?

First, get all the information you need. If confidentiality is important to you, ask about it: "Will you tell my parents about anything that goes on?" "Will you ask me about my other sexual partners, the other guys or girls I've been with?" "What kind of records do you keep?" "Who sees them?"

Make sure that the place you're approaching is offering what you need. "Do you offer treatment or only information?" "Can I get counseling through you?" "Can I come to see you with my boyfriend/girlfriend?" "When you say counseling, what exactly are you talking about?" "Do you have support groups I can join?"

Of course, find out what they expect from you. "What do you charge?" "What kind of payment do you accept—can I pay you in installments, or does it have to be all at once?" "Is there anything else you require that I should know about?"

Find out what their procedure is. "Do you have appointments, or do I just drop in?" "How long should I expect to wait?" "What are you going to ask me about?" If you get an appointment, make sure that you show up on time—otherwise, you may indeed find yourself waiting a long time. If you're visiting a drop-in facility, bring a book or magazine and maybe something to eat; let yourself have as pleasant an experience as possible.

Some people bring friends along with them, both so they'll get less nervous and so they'll have someone they can talk about the experience with afterward. A friend might also think of questions and suggestions that you might be too nervous or preoccupied to come up with at the time. If you want to bring a friend, find out if he or she is allowed to see the doctor or counselor with you, or if the person can only go as far as the waiting room.

Once you do see a "helper," be sure to be completely honest. The other person can't help you if he or she doesn't know what the situation is. If you don't like the way the person is treating you or talking to you, speak up. Make sure that you're being treated with care and respect—but also make sure that you're not just getting upset because you're hearing some painful or unpleasant facts that you'd rather not face right now. Some people find it helpful to take notes and get a phone number so that they can go home, process the information, and follow up on it later.

If you are getting treatment, be cooperative. Follow the instructions the doctor or health professional gives you. Pay attention to your health between visits, so you can tell your health-care worker what's going on with you. Demanding that a doctor or health professional respect you is a two-way street; you also need to show your respect for the other person by actively participating in your own treatment.

Whatever you do, give yourself a break. Getting help— whether treatment, information, counseling, or some combination—on sexual issues is a process that even some adults find difficult. You may feel only enormous relief that you're not alone with your concern—or you may feel worried, angry, frightened, paralyzed, or some other unpleasant emotion. Give yourself positive feedback for having the courage and the responsibility to take care of yourself in this way, and allow yourself all the time you need to take in the information that you're getting.

Coping with STDs isn't easy for anyone. But a person who is old enough to enjoy an intimate, sexual relationship with another is by definition old enough to take responsibility for his or her own health and that of his/her sexual partners. After reading this book and thinking it over, you may decide that you're not ready to take on this responsibility. You may choose to keep your romantic relationships on a less risky level, putting off more intimate and risky behavior for a future date. Or you may choose to approach your relationships with a new sense of responsibility and caring, making sure that you protect both yourself and your partner. Either way, coming to terms with these choices is part of growing up—and a part of being an adult that will be with you for the rest of your life.

7

Where to Find Help

The following organizations provide education, research, or referrals on sexually transmitted diseases.

Alan Guttmacher Institute
120 Wall Street
New York, NY 10005
212-248-1111

American Foundation for the Prevention of Venereal
  Disease
799 Broadway
Suite 638
New York, NY 10003
212-759-2069

Centers for Disease Control
National STD Hotline
1-800-227-8922

City of Toronto Public Health Department
277 Victoria Street
4th Floor
Toronto, Ontario M5B1W1
416-392-7420

CHOICE Hotline
215-592-0550

Gay Men's Health Crisis Hotline
212-807-6655

Health and Welfare Canada/Secretariat National Sur le
  SIDA (AIDS)
Edifice Jeanne Mance (Room 1742)
Tunney's Pasture
Ottawa, Ontario K1AOK9
613-952-5258

Ministere de la Sante et Services Sociaux
1088 Rue Raymond-Casgrain
Quebec, Quebec G152F4
418-648-2626

Planned Parenthood Federation of America
Educational Resources Clearinghouse
810 Seventh Avenue
New York, NY 10019
212-541-7800

Public Health Service
Centers for Disease Control
U.S. Public Health Service
1600 Clifton Rd., N.E.
Atlanta, GA 30333
404-639-3311

Sex Information and Education Council of the United States
130 West 42nd Street
25th Floor
New York, NY 10036–7901
212-819-9770

Tel-Med
212-434-3200
This phone service provides recorded information on a
variety of topics. To access STDs, press the following three-
digit numbers for the topics listed:

590	AIDS	715	Syphilis
716	Gonorrhea	708	Veneral Disease
270	Herpes	821	Chlamydia

VD National Hotline
800-227-8922

For Further Reading

The following books will provide further information on sexually transmitted diseases and sexuality.

Bell, Ruth. *Changing Bodies, Changing Lives: A Book for Teenagers on Sex and Relationships.* New York: Random House, Inc., 1988.

Bleich, Alan. *Coping with Health Risks and Risky Behavior.* New York: Rosen Group, 1990.

Boston Children's Hospital Staff. *What Teenagers Want to Know About Sex.* Boston: Little Brown and Co., 1988.

Carlson, Dale. *Loving Sex for Both Sexes: Straight Talk for Teenagers.* New York: Franklin Watts, 1979.

Core-Gebhart, Pennie, Susan Hart, and Michael Hart. *Living Smart: Understanding Sexuality in the Teen Years.* Fayetteville: University of Arkansas Press, 1991.

Daugirdas, John T. *STD: Sexually Transmitted Diseases including HIV/AIDS.* Hinsdale, IL: Medtext, 1992.

Landau, Elaine. *We Have AIDS.* New York: Franklin Watts, 1990.

Nourse, Alan E. *Sexually Transmitted Diseases.* New York: Franklin Watts, 1992.

———. *Teen Guide to AIDS Prevention.* New York: Franklin Watts, 1990.

———. *Teen Guide to Safe Sex.* New York: Franklin Watts, 1990.

Shaw, Diana. *What You Don't Know Can Hurt You.* Boston: Little Brown and Co., 1990.

Silverstein, Alvin, and Virginia Silverstein. *Learning about AIDS.* Hillside, NJ: Enslow Publications, 1989.

Watkins, James. *The Teen Sex Survival Manual: How to Cope in an R-Rated World.* Los Angeles: Bridge Publications, 1987.

Glossary

abdomen the area around the belly

abrasion scrape

AIDS acquired immune deficiency syndrome, the disease that results from a virus called HIV (see *HIV*) that destroys a body's ability to defend itself from disease

anal sex insertion of the penis into the anus and the rectum

anus rear opening

ARC AIDS-related complex (see *AIDS.*); the first series of diseases that a person infected with HIV (see *HIV*) might contract; later, the person might go on to get full-blown AIDS, which is generally associated with more severe diseases. Some researchers believe that there is no real difference between ARC and AIDS.

aroused sexually excited

bisexual a person who has sexual contact with people of both sexes

bladder the organ that holds urine (pee)

Caesarian section an operation to deliver a child; performed when the mother is having difficulty with labor or has an infectious disease in the genital area that might endanger the child

carrier someone who carries and can pass on a disease without necessarily having symptoms

celibate without any sexual partners

cervix the narrow canal in a woman's body leading from the vagina into the uterus

chancre (pronounced "shanker") an ulcer, pimple, or open sore that marks where syphilis entered the body and that can infect other people with syphilis

chlamydia a sexually transmitted disease that can cause infertility in women and may lead to arthritis or eye inflammations in men

circumcision the process of removing the foreskin from the penis, routinely done in infancy in some cultures or religions

clitoris a small external female sexual organ; the source of a woman's orgasm

contagious easy to pass on or to "catch," as in a *contagious* disease

contraceptive birth control (may also be called a *contraceptive device*)

cunnilingus kissing a woman's genitals

dental dam a rectangular piece of latex (rubbery plastic) that a woman can place lightly over her vagina during cunnilingus to block the transmission of blood and vaginal fluids to her partner while also blocking the transmission of blood from cuts or sores in the partner's mouth; can be bought at medical supply stores and some drug stores (it gets its name from being used by dentists to cover a person's mouth and isolate a single tooth.)

diaphragm a rubber cup, used with a spermicide as birth control; also seems somewhat effective in helping to prevent the transmission of disease

dilate open

douching the process of forcing water or other liquids up through the vagina, usually in order to clean that organ

ectopic pregnancy pregnancy that occurs when a fertilized egg implants in a woman's fallopian tube, rather than in her uterus, requiring surgery to save the woman's life and resulting in the loss of the embryo; often a result of chlamydia or PID; also known as a *tubal pregnancy*

ejaculation the process of a man releasing sperm from the penis, also known as *coming*

embryo an early form of an unborn child (the next form is the fetus)

erection a stiffened penis, ready for sexual intercourse

external outside, such as outside a person's body

fallopian tubes the tubes connecting a woman's uterus with her ovaries; where eggs are fertilized by sperm

feces bowel movements

fellatio kissing a man's genitals

fertility a man's ability to get a woman pregnant; a woman's ability to become pregnant and bear a child

fetus later form of an unborn child (after the embryo)

foreskin the flap of skin that covers the tip of the penis, removed during circumcision

frenulum the very sensitive roll of skin around the tip of the penis

ganglion the large part of a nerve in which a virus may continue to live

gay homosexual

genitals sexual organs

genital sex sexual activity involving the male and female genitals only: penis to vagina

glans penis the extremely sensitive tip or head of the penis

gonococcus the bacteria that causes gonorrhea

gonorrhea a sexually transmitted disease that can cause sterility in women and men

hemophiliac a person with a blood condition requiring frequent infusions with blood clotting factors

heterosexual a person who has sexual contact only with people of the opposite sex; also known as *straight*

heterosexuality sexual interest in people of the opposite sex

HIV human immunodeficiency virus, the virus that can give a person AIDS by destroying the immune system

HIV-negative having been tested for HIV and found to be not infected (also just called *negative*)

HIV-positive having been tested for HIV and found to be infected (also just called *positive*)

homosexual a person who has sexual contact only with people of the same sex; also known as *gay*

homosexuality sexual interest in people of the same sex

immunity the condition of being protected, or *immune*, from a disease; usually comes either from being vaccinated or from having had certain diseases before

incubation growth; the period during which a disease grows or develops inside a person before displaying symptoms

infectious capable of *infecting* someone, as with a disease

infertility the inability to have children

internal inside, such as inside a person's body

IUD intrauterine device, a birth-control device that fits inside a woman's uterus

IV drugs intravenous drugs; that is drugs that a person "shoots up" with a needle

jaundice a disease that turns the skin yellow; a symptom of hepatitis

labia majora the larger, outer lips that surround the opening to a woman's vagina

labia minora the smaller, inner lips that surround the opening to a woman's vagina

labaroscopy a procedure to investigate pelvic inflammatory disease in which a doctor inserts a viewing device through a slit made below the woman's navel

lesbian a woman who has sexual contact with other women

lubricate moisten

masturbation the process of touching one's own or another's sexual organs

menstruation the process of a woman's uterus losing its lining, which occurs every month if the woman's egg has not been fertilized; also called "getting a period"

miscarriage the accidental loss of an embryo or fetus during pregnancy

monogamous having only one sexual partner for an extended period

mutual masturbation when each member of a couple stimulates the other's sexual organs

nocturnal emissions also known as "wet dreams"; the process of a man ejaculating during his sleep

nonoxynol-9 a spermicide found in some contraceptive foams, some diaphragm creams and jellies, and as a lubricant on some condoms, apparently provides some protection against STDs

obstetrics the field of caring for pregnant women and delivering babies

oral sex contact between the mouth and the genitals; also known as cunnilingus (kissing the woman's genitals) and fellatio (kissing the man's genitals)

orgasm sexual climax, also known as *coming*; what a man reaches when he ejaculates

ovary the part of a woman's body that makes and stores eggs

ovulation the process or time of the month when an egg is released into the fallopian tubes

pelvis the lower part of the body, which includes internal and external sexual organs

Pap smear (cervical smear) a laboratory sample taken from the cervix, used to test for various STDs as well as cancer

penis one of a man's sexual organs; the organ that is inserted into another person during intercourse

peritonitis a life-threatening infection that might result from pelvic inflammatory disease

prostate a gland inside a man's body that produces some of the liquid in semen

PWA person with AIDS (see *AIDS*); often used to refer both to people who actually have AIDS or ARC (see *ARC*) and to people who are infected with HIV (see *HIV*) but have no other symptoms

rectum the intestine that extends into the body from the anus

scrotum the sack that holds a man's testes (or "balls")

semen the sticky fluid that men ejaculate, containing sperm, which is capable of fertilizing eggs and making a woman pregnant

seminal vesicle a tube in which the liquid that holds sperm is stored

shaft the length, or body, of the penis

sperm reproductive cells released by men to fertilize eggs and produce children

spermicide a cream or jelly that kills sperm, used with a diaphragm or in foam as a form of birth control; also seems useful in killing organisms that cause STDs

spinal cord the bundle of nerves that runs along the spine or back

sterility the inability to have children

stillbirth birth of a dead child

straight heterosexual

testes two of a man's external sexual organs, which produce sperm and the male hormone testosterone; "balls"

testosterone a male hormone

tubal pregnancy see *ectopic pregnancy*

transmitted passed along

ulcer sore

urethra the opening and canal leading to the bladder; the organ and opening through which men and woman urinate

urinary tract the canal between the bladder and the urethra through which men and women urinate

urination peeing

urine pee

uterus the woman's womb, where a baby grows during pregnancy

vagina one of a woman's internal sexual organs; the opening and canal that are entered by a penis during heterosexual intercourse

vas deferens a tube in a man's body that connects the prostate, urethra, and testes

vulva a woman's external sexual organs, including the labia majora, labia minora, and clitoris

INDEX